P9-CCW-762

Polymer Clay

Library of Congress Cataloging-in-Publication Data

Dean, Irene Semanchuk.
    Kids' crafts—polymer clay : 30 terrific projects to roll, mold & squish / Irene
Semanchuk Dean.— 1st ed.
        p. cm.
Includes index.
Summary: Provides step-by-step instructions for creating thirty objects from polymer
clay, as well as an explanation of the various tools required to make these and many
other decorative or fun products.
ISBN 1-57990-350-9
    1. Polymer clay craft—Juvenile literature. [1. Clay molding. 2. Handicraft.] I. Title.

TT297 .D37 2002
731.4'2—dc21

2002034212

10 9 8 7 6 5 4 3 2 1

First Edition

Editor: Joe Rhatigan

Art Director: Dana Irwin

Assistant Art Director: Hannes Charen

Photographer: Sandra Stambaugh

Cover Designer: Barbara Zaretsky

Illustrator: Orrin Lundgren

Production : Shannon Yokeley

Editorial Assistance: Delores Gosnell

Published by Lark Books, a division of
Sterling Publishing Co., Inc.
387 Park Avenue South, New York, N.Y. 10016

© 2003, Irene Semanchuk Dean

Distributed in Canada by Sterling Publishing,
c/o Canadian Manda Group, One Atlantic Ave., Suite 105
Toronto, Ontario, Canada M6K 3E7

Distributed in the U.K. by Guild of Master Craftsman Publications Ltd., Castle Place, 166
High Street, Lewes, East Sussex, England
BN7 1XU
Tel: (+ 44) 1273 477374, Fax: (+ 44) 1273 478606, Email: pubs@thegmcgroup.com, Web:
www.gmcpublications.com

Distributed in Australia by Capricorn Link (Australia) Pty Ltd.,
P.O. Box 704, Windsor, NSW 2756 Australia

If you have questions or com-
ments about this book, please contact:
Lark Books
67 Broadway
Asheville, NC 28801
(828) 253-0467

Manufactured in China

ISBN: 1-57990-350-9

Polymer Clay

30 Terrific Projects to Roll, Mold & Squish

Irene Semanchuk Dean

LARK KIDS' CRAFTS

Dedication

To Mom. Every mother as supportive as you deserves to have a book dedicated to her.

Acknowledgments

Thanks to Lark Books for their confidence in me and to my awesome editor Joe Rhatigan for his ideas and his perspective. Thanks to Sandra Stambaugh for her camera expertise and to Dana Irwin for wielding her design wand so well. Thanks to Sue for technical assistance, and to each of the contributing designers for their hard work and being willing to bend to accommodate my vision. Thanks and love to my husband Scott, for his support, encouragement, and general cheerleading.

I'd also like to thank the following kids for being our models and project testers:

Corrina Matthews

Andy Massey

Jacob Katz

Dylan Peifer

Leila Scogin

Elizabeth Lineback

Maggie Mathena

Alexandra Stromberg

Jasmine Villarreal

Natalie Ann Hopkins

Alexander Villarreal

Laurel Ashton

Dana Tarr

and

Jerita Villarreal (mad mom strikes!)

Contents

POLY WHAT?

Polymer clay, the most fun you'll ever have with a pliable, blendable polyvinyl chloride suspended in plasticizer.

HUH?

Okay, let me try again.

Polymer clay is a factory-made material that has been around since the 1950s or so (ancient history!). It was invented in Germany for making dolls, and it wasn't until around 20 years later that artists started making colorful beads and jewelry with it. Nowadays, people are doing all kinds of things with it, and more new ideas are being explored every day.

What will you be able to make? What a question! It's more like what *can't* you make with this clay. Put a hole in a piece of clay, and you've got the beginnings of a bead necklace.

Sculpt a miniature person, animal, or even a room complete with furniture, curtains, and a vase full of flowers. Cover jars, picture frames, light switch plates, and cabinet knobs. Make a weird bowl, a fat pen, a glow-in-the-dark mobile . . . the list is endless.

WHAT ELSE?

▶ Polymer clay doesn't dry out like earthen clay, so you can take your time creating with it—in other words, you can keep working until you're happy with your project.

▶ It comes in tons of colors, and you can create your own.

▶ You can bake your polymer clay projects

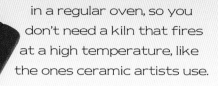

in a regular oven, so you don't need a kiln that fires at a high temperature, like the ones ceramic artists use.

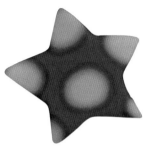

▶ The most important tools you'll need are your hands, and the rest of the tools you'll use are inexpensive and readily available.

I wrote this book to introduce the next generation of artists to this most excellent material. I've been creating with polymer clay for over 10 years now, and in fact, it's my full-time job. So, whether you've worked with polymer clay before, or you're hearing about it for the first time right here, this book will show you some pretty awesome things you can make that you probably never ever thought you could do.

One more thing: Please read the next chapter before starting on any of the projects. It will give you all the information you'll need to do every project in this book. Even if you've created with polymer clay before, take some time to check it out.

You've got 30 ideas here in this book. Use them as starting points, learn the techniques, create some fun stuff, and never be afraid to let your imagination take over. Ready? Turn the page.

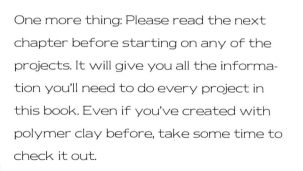

7

Start Here!

This chapter will take you through absolutely, positively everything you need to know to get started creating with polymer clay. So, read it before you try working on a project—especially since I refer to tools and techniques in the projects' instructions that are discussed right here.

SET UP YOUR WORK AREA

Artists and craftspeople usually have studios—separate rooms where they work on their projects. Most likely, you won't have that luxury. If you're lucky, however, you might have space in your bedroom or a corner of the basement you can clear out.

After you've found your "studio" space, you need a flat surface, such as an old table, to work on. Don't work on the nice dining room table—the clay can mess up the table's finish, and sharp tools will leave marks. (Someone's sure to get mad if this happens.)

You can work directly on a smooth ceramic tile or a metal cookie sheet so you can move your project directly to the oven when it's ready to be baked. Sometimes it's also handy to put a piece of typing paper down to work on, so it's easy to move the project. Experiment, and find out what works best for you.

Polymer Clay

There are two main sections to the instructions for each project in this book: What You Need and What You Do. (Pretty self-explanatory, eh?) The first line or two in the "What You Need" section tells you how much polymer clay you need and the colors used. If you don't like the colors listed, use different ones.

BUY YOUR CLAY

You can find polymer clay at any craft store and many toy stores. There are several different brands of clay available, and each one is slightly different in softness, strength, and color. You can experiment with different brands, or turn to page 112 for where to find more information on clay brands. You can mix together any of the brands to create new colors or degrees of workability (how soft or hard the clay is). Just make sure you mix them thoroughly. If you don't, the resulting clay may be weak.

Generally speaking, you can buy polymer clay in small, 2-ounce packages and larger, 1-pound bricks.

When shopping for clay:

▸ Make sure you don't buy clay that's hard.

▸ Learn which brand works best for you.

▸ Learn which stores or mail-order suppliers have the freshest clay.

WHERE TO STORE POLYMER CLAY

Besides putting it somewhere that your little brother can't get to it, it's important to keep your unbaked polymer clay away from heat and direct sunlight, both of which may make the clay stiffer and harder to work with. Cover your clay and work-in-progress with wax paper to keep them protected from dust and pet hair.

Tools and Other Stuff You Need....

Most of the stuff you need to work on the projects in this book can be found around your house; however, don't use kitchen utensils unless you have permission. Why not? Because you can't use any tools with food again once you've used them for polymer clay.

Without further delay, here's a list of tools and materials you might need:

ROLLING TOOLS

Of the four tools listed below, you only need one. Find the one you like to use best.

■ PRINTER'S BRAYER
This is perhaps the best tool for rolling out clay. You can use either a clear acrylic or black rubber brayer, though the clear acrylic seems to work better. You can find both at craft stores.

■ ACRYLIC ROD
This is a hollow or solid clear, plastic rod.

■ PLASTIC ROLLING PIN
As a last resort, you can use a plastic rolling pin to roll clay. Don't use a wooden one—it leaves marks on the clay, and the wood absorbs the plasticizer.

■ PASTA MACHINE
If there's an unused pasta machine around the house, ask if you can have it. It will make rolling sheets of clay a breeze. Pasta machines are also great for conditioning the clay (more about that in a minute), as well as for combining colors. Though not neces-

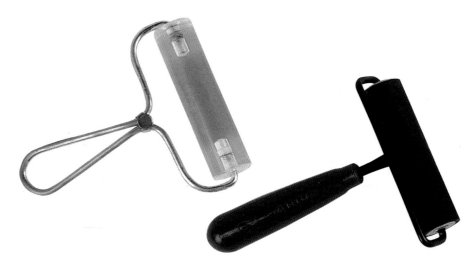

sary for the projects in this book, get your hands on one if you can. They're not terribly expensive, and they're fun and easy to use.

CUTTING TOOLS
....

You'll definitely need the first two of these tools. Please get an adult's help when learning how to use them, and always work carefully and slowly.

■ POLYMER CLAY CUTTING BLADE
This is a one-sided blade that's perfect for cutting sections of clay or for cutting canes. Look for one in the polymer clay section of a craft store.

■ CRAFT KNIFE
A common craft knife can also be used for cutting clay.

■ BUTTER KNIFE
It doesn't cut as well as either of the other tools; however, for some projects, a butter knife will perform all of your cutting needs just fine.

■ COOKIE CUTTERS
These can be used for making shapes out of sheets of clay. Buy your own cutters, or ask a parent whether or not you can take the ones gathering dust in the junk drawer. Cutters are also available at craft stores.

■ SMALL SHAPE CUTTERS
These are a lot like cookie cutters, but . . . smaller.

SCULPTING TOOLS

These tools push, nudge, and coax your clay into place. They fit in places where your pinky finger can't and can make anything from an interesting dotted design to a mouth, nostrils, or eyes.

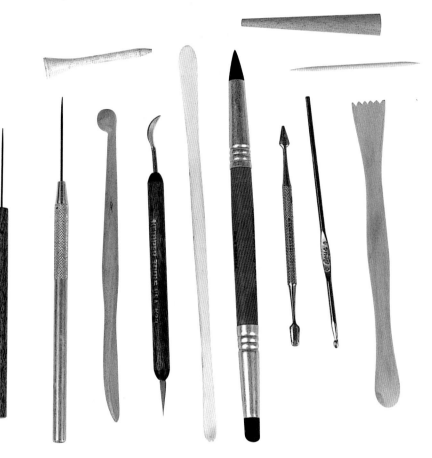

■ NEEDLE TOOL

In the ceramics or pottery section of a good craft store, you'll find a bunch of sculpting tools you can use. One of the handiest is called a needle tool. The long needle on the end of this tool is great for making holes for beads.

■ TOOTHPICK

Your next best sculpting friend is the toothpick. In many cases you can use a toothpick instead of a needle tool.

■ JUNK DRAWER ITEMS

You can also use junk drawer items such as a golf tee, cuticle shaper, crochet hook, bobby pin, paper clip, sewing needle, screw, bamboo skewer, fat knitting needle, and more to sculpt, incise, embellish, and decorate your clay.

TEXTURING TOOLS

Texturing tools are anything you can use to make patterned indentations or impressions in the clay. You can use rubber stamps, sandpaper, scraps of lace, window screen pieces, crumpled wax paper, the backside of a plastic dinosaur, interesting game 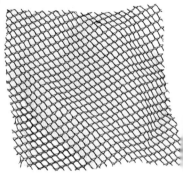 pieces, and even the clean bottom of a shoe.

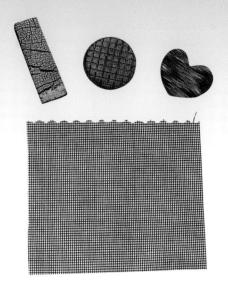

CERAMIC TILE, GLASS BAKING PAN, OR COOKIE BAKING SHEET

You need one of these to place your finished projects in the oven.

OVEN THERMOMETER

An inexpensive oven thermometer is a must, since oven temperatures are not always accurate, and polymer clay is very picky about the temperature.

POLYESTER BATTING OR PAPER

Most projects call for you to place your project on some polyester batting or a piece of paper for baking. (Don't worry, these materials won't burn at the low temperature at which you'll be baking the clay.) If you don't use them, your project may get a shiny flat spot where it was resting on the baking sheet or tile.

RELEASE AGENTS

When texturing clay, you'll sometimes need a very light application of either powder, cornstarch, or water to keep the texture from sticking to the clay (see page 17).

BAKING TOOLS

Baking your clay in a home oven is simple and one of the main reasons polymer clay is so popular. You need an oven or a toaster oven and the rest of the stuff listed here.

GLUES

Cyanoacrylate glue is an instant-bonding glue you can find at supermarkets and craft stores (for example, Instant Krazy Glue or Super Glue). You'll also need white craft glue (PVA), though make sure it's heat-resistant (Sobo Brand Craft and Fabric Glue works well). Check the polymer clay section of the craft store, or ask for help finding it. Also see page 112 for where to find more information on glue brands.

TOOLBOX

One of the best ways to keep all your tools together and make sure nobody uses them for anything else, is to find or buy a toolbox. This way, you'll know where everything is, and nobody will be tempted to use your cookie cutters to make cookies.

13

Important List of Safety Tips

Okay, we're almost ready to start working that clay, but first, even though polymer clay is certified non-toxic, there are a few safety tips you should be aware of:

▸ Never microwave your polymer clay!

▸ Don't snack while you're working with the clay. It's not a good idea to eat any of it, even very small amounts. Besides, you might get cheese puff crumbs in your project!

▸ Don't rub your eyes, pick your nose, etc. until you've washed the clay from your hands.

▸ To wash your hands, use regular hand lotion to break down the clay and make it easier to remove from your hands. Rub the lotion off with a terrycloth rag or paper towel, then wash with cold water, soap, and a nail brush to remove all residue.

▸ The tools you use for polymer clay should only be used for polymer clay. In other words, don't return the pasta machine to the kitchen cabinet once you've run clay through it.

▸ Ventilate well when baking, and don't breathe the fumes. Be sure to use an oven thermometer to prevent burning. Open a window and turn on a fan if you do end up burning the clay.

▸ Polymer clay should never be used to make anything to eat or drink out of. No ashtrays or incense burners, either!

Working with the Clay

The instructions for each project tell you exactly what to do in order to design your own polymer clay creation.

I've also included lots of step-by-step photographs to show you what I'm writing about. But before you start working on the steps, there are a few more things you need to consider.

FIGURING AMOUNTS

Most brands of polymer clay are conveniently marked so you can cut them into equal portions. If you buy blocks that aren't marked, don't worry. Since most amounts listed in the "What You Need" section are approximate, you can usually eyeball how much clay you'll need and be okay.

CONDITIONING THE CLAY

Though some of the polymer clays are kind of soft and workable right out of the package, it's still necessary to squish and squeeze it before you use it. This is called *conditioning*, and not only does it make the clay softer, more malleable, and hence easier to use, but it will also make your finished project stronger. Conditioning ensures that the plasticizer (the stuff that makes the clay soft) is evenly distributed throughout the clay. A project made with unconditioned clay might be weak and could break.

■ HOW TO CONDITION YOUR CLAY

‣ Use your hands, and squeeze about a 1-ounce block until you can roll it into a snake.

‣ Fold the snake a few times; roll it out again, fold again. Try not to get any air bubbles in your clay when you do this.

‣ Roll and fold until you can pull the ends of the clay and it stretches instead of breaks.

‣ If you're also mixing colors, conditioning is the perfect time to do it since you use the same process for both.

■ USING A PASTA MACHINE

Conditioning with a pasta machine is a cinch! Most models come with a clamp you can use to secure the machine to your work table.

‣ Cut up your block of clay into slabs no thicker than ¼ inch. If the clay is too thick, you'll damage the machine.

‣ Set the machine at its thickest setting (#1 on most models), and roll your clay through.

‣ Fold the sheet and repeat. Keep doing this until the clay stretches when pulled.

‣ When you put the folded clay through the pasta machine, be sure the fold isn't on the top edge, or you'll trap air in the fold.

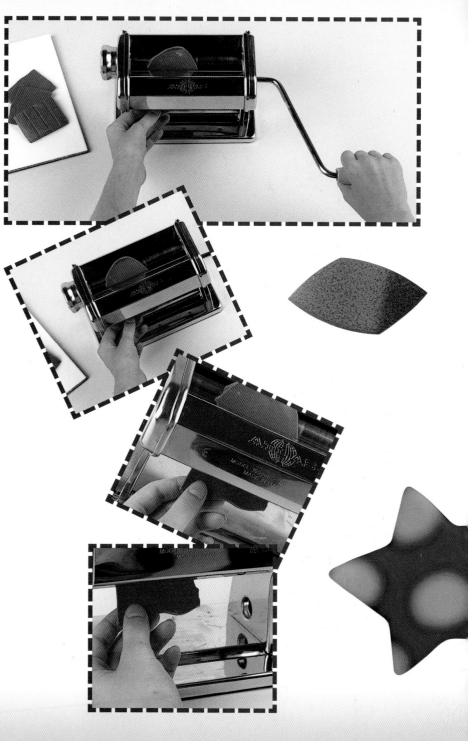

CHOOSING & MIXING COLORS

Although polymer clay comes in a huge variety of colors, if you can't find the color you want, you can mix clays to create nearly any color. You can combine colors randomly, adding a pinch of this and a smidgen of that until you've got a color you like, or follow these guidelines for creating your own color recipes:

▸ Combine yellow and blue to get green.

▸ Combine red and blue to get purple.

▸ Combine yellow and red to get orange.

▸ To darken a color, add a small amount of black.

▸ To lighten a color or make it look more pastel, start with white and add color to it.

▸ If you vary the proportions of the colors in the mixture, you'll get colors such as bluish green or pale orange.

ROLLING OUT YOUR CLAY

In the "What You Need" section, whenever you need a rolling tool it will say "Rolling tool or pasta machine."

Experiment with rollers, if you can, until you have one you like best. Just about every

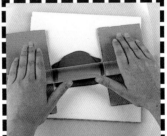

project will tell you to first roll your conditioned clay into a sheet. That means taking a small, thick clump of clay and rolling it thin, as you would cookie dough. Sometimes I like to put the clay between two pieces of wax paper to keep the clay from sticking to the roller. Then, it's a simple matter of rolling until the clay is the thickness and size you want. Roll back and forth and then side to side; flip it over and roll some more. This will result in a more even sheet. To roll out a 1/8-inch thick sheet of clay, first place two pieces of cardboard on either side of the clay you're about to roll.

■ ROLLING WITH A PASTA MACHINE

Many of the sheets you'll roll will be 1/8-inch thick (the thickest setting on the machine). That's about the same thickness as a piece of cardboard.

Always start rolling at the thickest setting, and if you need a thinner sheet, set the machine one or two notches thinner each time. If you go from thickest to thinnest right away, you'll damage the machine. Refer to page 15 for further instructions.

CUTTING THE CLAY

After rolling out your clay, you'll sometimes be asked to cut it. The tools listed on page 11 are all you need to do all the cutting in this book. Make sure you're always careful with these tools, and don't leave them around the house for your far less responsible younger siblings to play with.

■ USING A CRAFT KNIFE

A craft knife is helpful for cutting simple designs. Hold the craft knife firmly in one hand, and press the tip of the knife into the clay. Slowly drag the knife to make a cut.

■ USING A POLYMER CLAY CUTTING BLADE

This tool is good for cutting canes (more on that on page 19) and cutting straight lines in the clay. Since it only has one sharp edge, you can hold it by its blunt edge, and you won't hurt your hand. See the photo below for the best way to hold it.

COOL TRICKS

The rest of the project instructions will show you what to do next. If the instructions mention a technique you're not familiar with, simply turn back to this section, and read the instructions for that technique. You'll learn lots of different ways to decorate your clay projects. Some are simple, and some require a little more patience and practice. Here they are, in no particular order.

■ TEXTURING

Texturing creates fun surfaces for your polymer clay projects, so they feel and look great. Do you want your clay to look sort of rough? Press sandpaper into the surface. Looking for a geometric pattern? Use a small piece of window screen or lace. Start collecting cool texturing tools in your toolbox.

■ KEEPING THE CLAY FROM STICKING TO YOUR TEXTURE

Sometimes the polymer clay will stick to the texturing item or even to your tools. When that happens, you can spread a little cornstarch on the clay with your fingertip. You can also just dip your fingertip into a bowl of water, and rub it onto the clay. Either way will allow the texture to do its job without sticking.

■ MARBLING

Marbling is something we do with polymer clay almost instinctively. Twist and turn two or more colors together until you like how it looks. Don't overdo it, or the colors will start to blend together, and you might get mud.

■ EMBEDDING

Embedding simply means sticking objects into the clay. You can push them in all the way or leave them sticking out a bit. There are so many things you can embed into your clay projects, it would be impossible to list them all here. If you don't think your object will stick, make a small indentation in the clay, dab a little bit of heat-resistant PVA glue on the object, and gently place the object into the indentation. If objects fall out

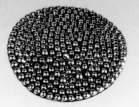

after baking, simply place a dot of cyano-acrylate glue on the object and try again. If you think the object might melt when baking, just glue it in place afterwards.

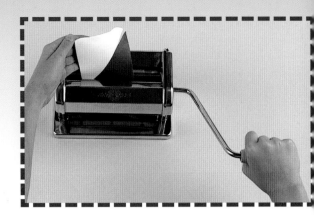

between each pass through the machine.. The colors will blend smoothly from one to another, and you can use this blended sheet to add some extra pizzazz to your projects.

■ ONLAY

When you add small pieces of clay to the surface of another piece of clay and leave them sticking up a little, it's called *onlay* or *appliqué*. You can use cut-out shapes, tiny balls you roll between your fingers, or slices from canes. You can build up layers, too. Press the pieces of onlaid clay enough to make them stick, but not so much that you squish them.

■ COVERING SURFACING

Sometimes you may want to cover a surface or object that polymer clay doesn't want to stick to, such as wood or metal. It's easy to fix that! Apply a thin coat of heat-resistant PVA glue to the wood or metal, allow it to dry, and put your clay on that. Polymer clay will stick to this glue even when it has dried completely, which certainly makes it easier to handle.

■ SKINNER BLEND

You need a pasta machine for this trick. Cut triangles from sheets of two colors of clay, and fit them next to each other. Run them through the pasta machine many times, and always fold the sheet from bottom to top

■ CANEWORKING

Basically, a polymer clay cane is a tube or log of clay that, when assembled just right, has the same image running all the way

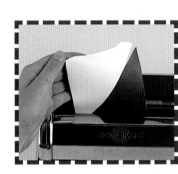

through it when you slice it. Caneworking is a popular and easy way to add decoration to your projects. You can buy pre-made canes, but it's much more fun to make your own.

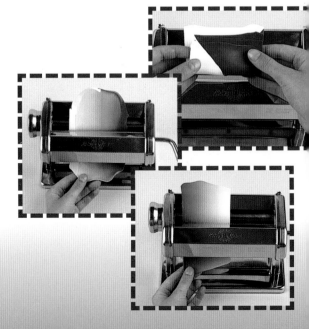

18

■ Cane Basics

▸ The bigger you make the cane, the more slices you get.

▸ Canes can be square, triangular, round, or even irregularly shaped.

▸ When building a cane, make sure to use the same brand of clay throughout. This will ensure that the clay is the same consistency, and your slices won't get distorted when you cut them.

▸ If you can, allow a cane to rest overnight after building it. The clay gets warm from all that squashing and rolling, and if you try to cut slices right away, they might be distorted. Another trick is to put a warm cane in the refrigerator for 30 minutes.

▸ To make a cane longer and smaller in diameter (called *reducing*), slowly and gently roll it back and forth with deliberate motions. To minimize distortion, make sure you reduce the cane evenly from one end to the other. (If the cane is too long to handle, cut off sections small enough to roll evenly.)

▸ To reduce a square cane, use a brayer to roll from the center of the cane to each end. Continue this process, and occasionally flip it over so that the direction of the pressure you're applying is even on all ends.

■ Jellyroll Cane

This is a simple cane that looks great. Roll out rectangular sheets of two or more different colors of clay. Stack the sheets, gently press them together to eliminate air bubbles, and trim the edges so that they're all the same size. Turn one of the short ends of the stack upward, and roll up the stack to form a tube.

■ Bull's-Eye Cane

Use your hands to shape a single color of clay into a log. Roll out a sheet of a contrasting color, and cut it as wide as the log is long. Make a clean, straight cut along one edge of the sheet, and press the log gently into place along this edge. Carefully roll up the log inside the sheet. Where the edge presses into the sheet, roll it back a little, and you'll see the mark left by the edge. Slice away the excess clay at that mark, and finish rolling the log (the edges will butt together). Repeat this to add as many rings as you like.

19

▪ Striped Cane

Stack together two or more sheets of clay in contrasting colors. Cut the stack in half, and place one half on top of the other. Repeat this process until you have the number of stripes you want. If needed, reduce the stack by rolling the top of it with a brayer.

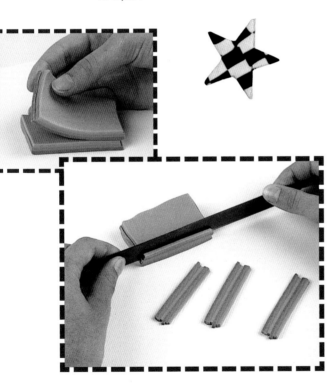

▪ Checkerboard Cane

Use a rolling tool or pasta machine to roll two sheets of contrasting colors to the same thickness. Press them together gently, and trim them so that the edges are even. Cut this slab into strips, and flip over every other strip. Cut this slab in half crosswise. Stack one section on top of the other to create a checkerboard pattern.

■ Cutting a Cane

You've built your cane, and now it's time to cut it. The best tool for the job is the polymer clay cutting blade (page 11). To prevent smears, clean your blade with rubbing alcohol or a baby wipe cloth after every few slices. Rotate the cane a quarter turn before making your next slice, so that you're not applying pressure to the same side, which could result in a distorted slice. If your slices are smeared, your cane may be too warm, so allow it to rest. Set the cane in the refrigerator until it's cool enough to slice cleanly.

CURING YOUR PROJECTS

No, you're not trying to make your sick polymer clay feel better. Curing or baking your clay means applying heat to your finished polymer clay project in order to make it hard. As I mentioned in the introduction, one of the great things about polymer clay is that you can bake it in the oven. According to the manufacturers, it's safe to bake in your home oven, but you should still follow some basic safety guidelines.

■ HOW TO BAKE

First, get a parent's permission to use the oven. Promise that you'll clean it when you're done (more on that below). Second, get an oven thermometer, and use it. Next, you need a metal tray, glass dish, or smooth ceramic tile to bake your projects on. Remember to put a piece of paper, polyester batting, or even a wadded-up piece of cotton cloth on the baking tray to avoid a flat shiny mark on the clay.

Polymer clays bake at approximately 275°F. If the temperature is not hot enough, the polymer molecules will not fuse properly, and your finished piece will be weak. If it's too hot, your project will burn, and you'll gag on the fumes that result and send everyone out of the house until the smoke clears.

For best results, preheat the oven first using the oven thermometer as a guide.

Always refer to the polymer clay manufacturer's instructions for what temperature best suits the clay you're using. The project instructions will give you approximate times for how long to bake the clay.

■ TOASTER OVEN

You can always check the local resale shops for a toaster oven if you want to get an oven just for polymer clay. Be sure to use an oven thermometer in a toaster oven, since the oven's temperature gauge is usually inaccurate. It's also good to create a tent with aluminum foil (see photo below) when using a toaster oven to protect your clay from the intense heat at the top of the toaster oven.

■ OTHER OVEN THOUGHTS

‣ Be sure to ventilate well by keeping windows open or using the oven's exhaust fan.

‣ You can "tent" the baking tray you put your projects on with aluminum foil (see photo). The foil will allow the heat to cure your projects but will keep any residue from reaching the sides of the oven.

‣ Be sure to bake for the full amount of time recommended for each project.

‣ While it's possible to burn the clay by baking it at too hot a temperature, it's okay to bake longer than the instructions say.

■ CLEANING THE OVEN

You can safely remove any polymer clay residue from your oven by wiping the inside of the cool oven with a little baking soda on a damp sponge, then wiping with a wet sponge or rag. Hundreds, maybe thousands, of people bake polymer clay in their ovens and never clean them afterward; however, it's my advice that it can't hurt to be extra safe. If you don't have a dedicated oven, "tent" your clay or wipe down the interior as described.

FURTHER DECORATING CURED PROJECTS

Just because your project is baked, doesn't mean you have to be through. You can still paint your project. (Use acrylic paints.) You can also use gel pens. Use cyanoacrylate glue to stick objects to your baked projects. With this glue, ventilate well. Squirt a little bit of glue onto wax paper, and apply it with a toothpick. Since I started doing it this way, I hardly ever glue my fingers together. And, if you want to add some shine to your finished projects, you can buy special polymer clay varnishes. Don't use nail polish! It will ruin your project.

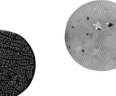

Well, that's about it. You're ready now.

22

Good luck! Have fun! And return to this chapter if you need help!

Now Presenting, without Further Delay...
the Projects

The best thing about polymer clay is that the more you play with it, the more comfortable you'll feel using the tools, squashing the clay, and making stuff. Sure, your first project may not look like the one in the book, but don't freak out. Working with polymer clay takes a little practice, and I don't want you to get discouraged if your first polymer clay beetle doesn't look totally awesome. Try it again. Make a bunch of beetles. Then, compare the first one to your most recent one. Not bad, eh? And if you think you've got a better way to do something, go for it. Experiment with colors, tricks, and techniques. It won't be long before you're coming up with your own project ideas.

Novel Knobs

Once you make one of these, you won't be able to stop. Your family's cabinets and dressers will never, ever be the same!

What You Need

- Polymer clay: ½ ounce each in various colors*

- Wooden cabinet knobs

- Heat-resistant PVA glue

- Rolling tool

- Polymer clay cutting blade

- Craft knife

- 1-inch circle cutter

* Quantity depends on how many knobs you're making. The instructions below are for one knob.

What You Do

1 Use your fingers to coat the cabinet knobs with a thin layer of the heat-resistant glue. Let the glue dry completely—this won't take more than 20 minutes or so.

2 Roll a sheet of clay that's long enough to wrap around the base of the knob. The clay doesn't have to cover the top of the knob—you'll decorate that later.

3 Cut one straight edge of the sheet of clay, and press it onto the side of the knob. Wrap the clay around the base of the knob, and press it to the knob as you wrap it (photo 1).

4 Trim the clay with the craft knife where it starts to overlap, and smooth the seam with your fingertip. The top of that strip of clay you wrapped around the knob will extend partway over the edge onto the top of the knob. Smooth it with your fingers to flatten it onto the top of the knob (photo 2). Set the knob aside for a moment.

5 Roll a small sheet of clay in a contrasting color. Use the circle cutter to cut out (you guessed it) a circle. Place this on top of the knob, and press gently from the center out toward the edges to eliminate air bubbles (photo 3). This should overlap the edges of the clay you wrapped around the base of the knob.

6 Now all the interesting possibilities come in! You can roll a thin strand of another contrasting color of clay, and form a peace sign on the top of the knob. Several short, tapered snakes of clay can become flower petals (photo 4). You can use skinny snakes of clay to "draw" on the top of the knob, or add some cane slices (see page 19). It's probably a good idea to avoid any designs that have pieces sticking out, since they might get broken off when the knobs are used. Bake the knob for 30 minutes.

Marblelous Ornaments

Play with colors, shapes, textures, and sizes to create holiday decorations, gift tags, invitations, or even something for the family car's rearview mirror.

What You Need

- Polymer clay:
  At least two colors
  that look nice
  together
- Rolling tool
- Texturing tools
  (see page 12)
- Cookie cutters
- Plastic drinking straw
- Yarn or ribbon

What You Do

1 Roll the colors into snakes. The more you twist, the more striped your ornament will be (photo 1). Be careful not to twist too much, or you'll lose the swirling effect.

2 Roll the twisted clay into a thin sheet, and texture it (photo 2).

3 Decide where on the sheet is the nicest area of swirly colors, and cut out your ornament with a cookie cutter (photo 3).

4 Remove the excess clay, and set it aside. Press the plastic drinking straw into the clay shape where you want to tie your string for hanging (photo 4). Remove that little circle of clay.

5 Bake for 20 to 30 minutes. When the ornament has baked and cooled, loop a piece of string through the hole, and tie a knot.

1

2

3

4

Makin' Faces Switch Plates

H ere are some funny faces you can make without getting in any trouble.

What You Need

▸ Polymer clay:
1 ounce purple
½ ounce light green
Small amounts of white, red, green, and turquoise
Slices from a simple cane (optional)

▸ Rolling tool

▸ Plastic or metal light switch plate

▸ Texturing tools (see page 12)

▸ Craft knife

▸ Pencil or golf tee

▸ Brightly colored craft wire

What You Do

1 Roll out a thin sheet of purple clay. Lay it onto the front of the switch plate, and smooth from the center to the edges to work out any air bubbles. Add some texture to the clay if you want (photo 1). Flip the plate over, and trim the excess clay from the back.

2 Cut out the toggle hole in the center of the switch plate. Use the pencil or golf tee to poke the clay out of the screw holes.

3 Now's the fun— adding the face parts! (When decorating, make sure not to cover the holes you just cut out.) Cut two almond shapes from a sheet of white clay for eyes. Place these just above the toggle hole. Flatten two small balls of turquoise clay for the irises. Use a very thin strip of purple along the top edge of the eyes for eyelids (photo 2).

4 For lips, roll two mar-ble-sized balls of red clay into short, thick logs, about 1½ inches long.

Taper the ends of the logs so that each lip is much wider in the middle. Roll the edge of a pencil along the center of one lip to create the indenta-tion in the middle of the upper lip. Place the lips together as shown (photo 3), then place them onto the switch plate.

5 Coil the wire around the pen-cil. Slide it off, and spread the coils out by pulling on each end slightly. Cut this into three or more pieces. Straighten ½ inch of one end of each coil, and press this end into the switch plate on the upper edge (see photo 4 on page 32).

6 Roll a sheet of green clay, and cut it into a lopsided rectangle for a hat (see photo 5). Place this at the top of the switch plate, covering where the wire is inserted. Decorate along the edge with the tip of the golf tee or needle tool. Trim the edges of the hat.

7 Add some hat decoration by cutting some leaf shapes from green polymer clay. Use some cane slices to represent dangling earrings, too (photo 5). Bake for 20 minutes.

Witch's Cauldron

Y ou can cook up count-less variations of this simple pot—perfect for paper clips, knickknacks, earrings, etc. But not lizards.

33

- ▸ Polymer clay:
  3 ounces fuchsia
  1 ounce each of
  yellow and green
- ▸ Jar lid or other flat
  object
- ▸ Large and small star
  cutters
- ▸ Cyanoacrylate glue

What You Do

1 Roll a 2-ounce piece of fuchsia clay into a smooth, round ball. Poke your thumb into it, and stop about halfway down. Hold the clay in one hand, and put the thumb of your other hand inside the hole. Gently enlarge the hole by pressing the clay between your thumbs and fingers, and let the sides stay curved inward toward the top (photo 1).

2 The bottom and sides will become thinner as you enlarge the hole. Work slowly and patiently for best results. If the bowl becomes too lopsided or thin, you can roll the clay back into a ball and start over. Set it aside when you're done.

3 To make the feet, roll three marble-sized balls of fuchsia, and place them about 1 inch apart. Press down on all three balls at the same time with the jar lid to flatten them (photo 2). The balls should squish toward each other and touch in the middle.

4 Center the bottom of the pot on top of the three feet, and press from the inside of the pot to make sure the feet stick (photo 3).

5 Roll the yellow clay into a thin sheet. Cut seven stars with the small cookie-cutter, and place them evenly around the widest part of the pinch pot. Roll seven tiny balls of green clay, and put one in the middle of each star (photo 4). Bake the pot for 30 minutes.

6 Roll the remaining green clay into a smooth ball, and use the jar lid to press the clay into a flat disk that's larger than the opening on the pinch pot.

7 Hold the cooled pinch pot upside down, and press its opening onto the green disk (photo 5). Rotate the pinch pot a bit to leave a slight indentation in the green clay, and remove the pot. This indentation will help the lid fit perfectly on the pot.

8 Turn the lid over, cut a large star from the remaining yellow clay, and center it on the green disk.

9 Roll the remaining fuchsia clay into a long cone shape with a pointy end (photo 6). Press the bottom of the cone in the middle of the yellow star, and curl the pointy end. Bake the lid for 30 minutes.

Doughnut Designs

Now presenting: the incredible, inedible doughnut pendant.

What You Need

- Polymer clay:
  Black and white jelly-roll cane (see page 19), ½ inch in diameter
  1 ounce fuchsia

- Polymer clay cutting blade

- Bamboo skewer

- Fat knitting needle

- 3 feet of 1 mm black rubber or leather cord

What You Do

1 Squeeze the black and white jellyroll cane into a triangle (photo 1). Cut off 2 inches of the cane, and set it aside. Gently pull and squeeze the remaining cane, keeping the triangular shape, until it is about ¼ inch high. Set it aside.

2 Roll the fuchsia clay into a smooth, seamless ball. Hold the ball between the palms of your hands, and press your palms together gently to flatten the ball into a thick disk.

3 Use the skewer to poke a hole through the center of the disk. Turn the disk over, and poke the skewer back through the hole, using a circular motion to enlarge the hole. When the hole is large enough, insert the knitting needle, still using the circular motion to enlarge the hole until it's about ½ inch in diameter (photo 2). The disk should now look like a doughnut.

4 With the cutting blade, cut seven slices from the large triangle cane and 14 slices from the smaller cane. Position the slices in three circular rows as shown in photo 3. If you place the slices very lightly on the doughnut, you'll be able to pick them up and reposition them so they're evenly spaced around the hole.

5 When the slices are positioned the way you want them, press lightly on each slice to stick it to the doughnut. Don't mash them; just press enough so they stick. Bake for 30 minutes. When the project is cool, thread and knot the rubber or leather cord through the hole.

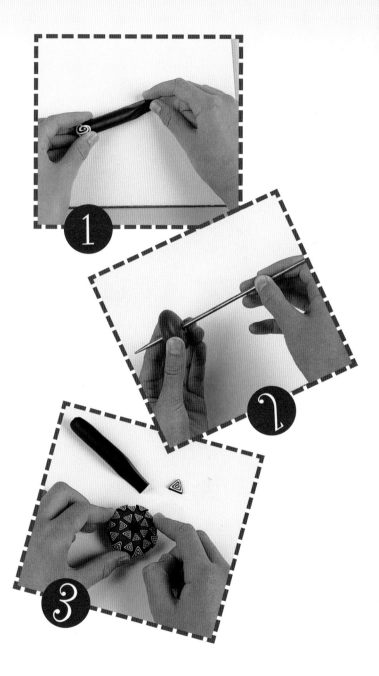

Pushpinzzzzzzzzz

P eople are sure to buzz around your bulletin board if you make and use these bee-utiful pushpins.

What You Need

- Polymer clay:
  ¼ ounce each of fluorescent, black, and glow-in-the-dark*
- Pushpin
- Rubbing alcohol
- Paper towel
- Rolling tool
- Craft knife
- Polyester batting or paper towel

*Amounts indicated here are for one bee.

What You Do

1 Clean one pushpin with a little bit of rubbing alcohol on a paper towel. Roll the fluorescent clay into a ¼-inch-thick sheet. Cut a strip from this sheet wide enough to fill in the middle area of the pushpin. Place the clay around the middle of the pin, and press it into place (photo 1). Trim with the craft knife so that the clay doesn't overlap. Set this aside.

2 Roll some thin spaghetti-sized snakes, some in the same fluorescent color you used to cover the pushpin, and some in black. Cut them into pieces about as long as your index finger.

3 Line the snakes up, alternating black and fluorescent, until you have a strip about ½ inch wide. Gently flatten them slightly with the rolling tool until they stick to each other (photo 2).

4 Trim the strip until it's as wide as the body of the pushpin. Cut one edge straight. Place it onto the body of the pushpin, and roll it so the stripes go around the body all the way without overlapping. Press the stripes in place (photo 3).

5 Very gently smooth the seam. Don't worry if you can't make it perfectly smooth—you can put the wings there later to cover it. With your fingers, round off the top and bottom to make the body into an egg shape (photo 4).

6 To finish the body, roll a piece of black clay into a ball the size of a pea. Cut it in half. Insert the point of the stinger, I mean the pin, into the flat side of one piece of the black clay, and push the clay up the pin until it touches the striped body (see photo 5 on page 40). Press it to adhere, and smooth where you need to.

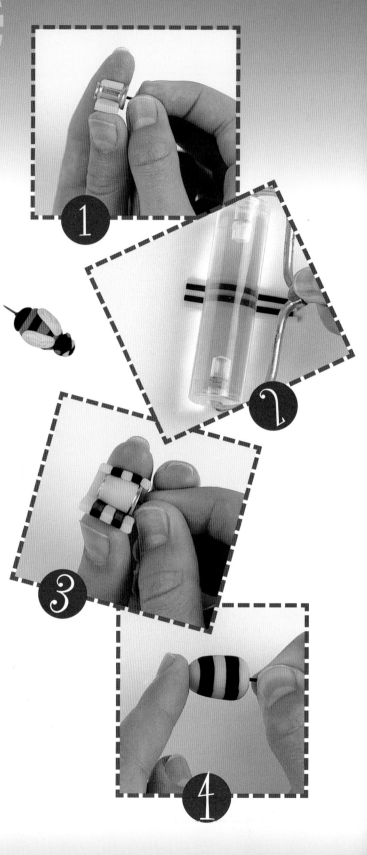

7 Use the other half of the pea-sized ball you made in step 6, and roll it into a ball for the head. Stick it to the body (photo 6). Use glow-in-the-dark and black clay to make eyes, a mouth, and antennae. press them onto the body. Bake the bee on a piece of polyester batting or wadded paper towel for 30 minutes. For more bees, simply use different colors of clay.

8 Roll two pea-sized, glow-in-the-dark teardrop shapes for the wings. Flatten them slightly, and

Window Clings

L iquid polymer clay is a cool material that's just what it sounds like. Window Clings are also just what they sound like. Also very cool.

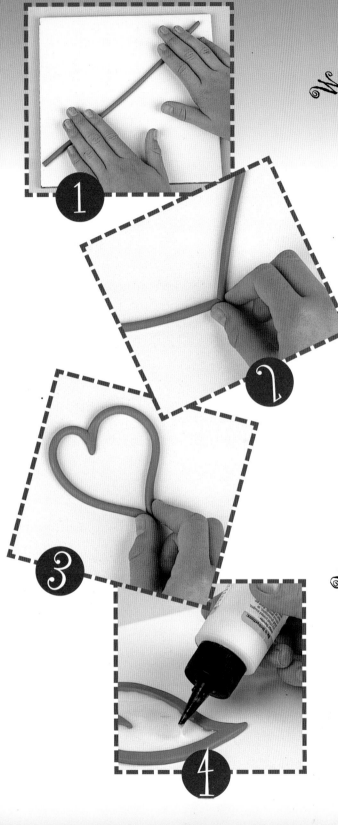

What You Need

- Polymer clay: ½ ounce turquoise*
- Translucent liquid polymer clay
- Craft knife
- Smooth glazed ceramic tile
- Rolling tool
- Craft stick or toothpick
- Glitter
- Aluminum foil (optional)

*Amount indicated here is for one window cling.

What You Do

1 Roll a snake of turquoise clay about 8 inches long and a bit thinner than a pencil. Try to make the snake an even thickness for the whole length (photo 1). This snake will be the frame for the window cling.

2 Cut the snake into two equal-sized pieces. Slice each end of both snakes at an angle. Join the ends together as shown in photo 2, and lightly smooth the seam. This is the center point of the heart. Gently press the center point down onto the ceramic tile just enough to hold it in place.

3 Form the snake pieces into the heart shape, and pinch and smooth the clay together (photo 3). Roll over the frame every so slightly. You just want the frame to stick completely to the tile; you don't want to squish it flat.

4 Squeeze a small amount of the liquid clay inside the heart along the frame's edge, and then add a small amount in the center. Just use enough liquid clay to fill the inside area of the heart (photo 4). Be careful not to go over the edges.

5 Use the craft stick or toothpick to slowly move the liquid clay around until the inside area is completely filled in and touching all sides of the clay. Let this sit for 15 minutes so it will level out.

6 Sprinkle a tiny pinch of glitter on to the top of the liquid clay (photo 5). Don't stir the liquid clay, no matter how tempting it seems. Add glitter to the frame as well (photo 6).

7 Time to bake! When you carry the tile to the oven, be sure to keep it flat so the liquid clay won't run over the edges of the frame. Bake in a preheated oven for 15 minutes at the manufacturer's recommended temperature. Liquid polymer clay is pretty stinky when baking, so make a tent with aluminum foil, as shown on page 21, and make sure you open a window. After 15 minutes, shut the oven off, and leave the tile in the oven to cool for an hour.

8 When cool, peel the cling from the tile slowly. Your cling can now be pressed to a clean window or mirror!

LIQUID POLYMER CLAY

* Comes in white and translucent, but you can color it by stirring in a drop or two of oil paint.

* Can be used as a glue to stick two pieces of clay together. Even if the two pieces of clay have been baked, you have to bake them again so the liquid clay hardens.

* Creates a very noticeable odor when it's baking. Be sure to ventilate well!

* Can be dribbled, brushed, or smeared on a project to add decoration.

It's a Hold-Up

...**F**or favorite photos, messages, and notes, that is. Make your holder as big or small as you want, and decorate it to your heart's content.

- ▸ Polymer clay:
  2 ounces pale blue
  1 ounce pearl
  Less than ½ ounce
     each of blue, pink,
     purple, green, yellow,
     and black

- ▸ Rolling tool

- ▸ Coarse sandpaper or
  kitchen scrubbing pad

- ▸ Craft knife

- ▸ Templates on page 108

- ▸ 16- or 18-gauge craft
  wire (for holders)

- ▸ 22- or 24-gauge craft
  wire (optional)

- ▸ Wire cutters

- ▸ Small pliers

- ▸ Ruler

- ▸ Cyanoacrylate glue

- ▸ Assorted beads
  (optional)

What You Do

1 To make the base, roll the pale blue clay into a ball, and then flatten the bottom to create a dome. Texture it with the sandpaper or scrubbing pad (photo 1).

2 Flatten the yellow, pink, and purple clay into ⅛-inch-thick sheets.

3 Use the templates on page 108 to cut out the shapes to decorate the base. Press the shapes firmly to the base. Then roll some small pieces of black for the butterfly bodies, and place them on the wings. (photo 2).

4 For the grass, roll green clay into a thin sheet, and cut it into small strips. Then cut tiny slits in these strips with your craft knife. Gently separate these "blades" when pressing the strips to the base (photo 3).

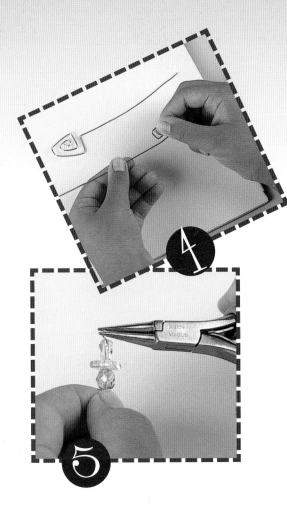

5 Use a piece of wire to poke holes in the top of the base where you plan to add "holders" later. Make sure the holes are about 1/2 inch deep. Bake the base for at least 20 minutes.

6 While that's baking, cut a 10-inch piece of craft wire for each hole you made in the base. Use the pliers to curl one end of each wire into a small, simple shape. Hold this part between your thumb and index finger, and continue curling into a spiral, following the same shape and enlarging as you go around, as shown in photo 4. You should bend the wire around at least three times to make an effective holder.

7 When you've made it the size you want, bend the rest of the wire away from the shape at a 90° angle. Insert the wires into the baked and cooled base, checking for length. Remove the wire, and trim the excess, if there is any.

8 Apply the glue to the end of each wire, and reinsert it into the holes on the base.

9 Want to add some dangles? Cut the thinner wire into short lengths. Curl one end into a small spiral or zigzag shape, and add some beads. Trim all but 1/4 inch of the wire, and use your pliers to turn it into a loop. Open the loop slightly to add the bead to the wire holder, and then squeeze closed gently with the pliers (photo 5).

Accordion Book

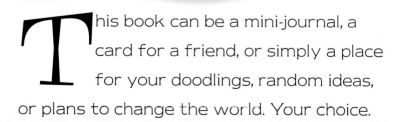

This book can be a mini-journal, a card for a friend, or simply a place for your doodlings, random ideas, or plans to change the world. Your choice.

1

2

What You Need

▸ Polymer clay: 4 ounces of any color

▸ Rolling tool

▸ Rubber stamps and ink pad

▸ Decorating chalks or pastels

▸ Cotton swabs

▸ Texturing tools (see page 12)

▸ Craft knife

▸ Ruler

▸ Large piece of thick paper*

▸ Scissors

▸ Glue stick

▸ Decorative printed paper or wrapping paper (optional)

*Available at craft and art supply stores.

What You Do

1 Decide how big you want your book to be. Roll a sheet of clay about 1/8 inch thick, and cut it to the size you want the cover to be.

2 For the front cover, ink the rubber stamp, and stamp the image into the center of the polymer clay sheet. Press firmly, but not so hard that the stamp squashes into the clay (photo 1).

3 Once the ink is completely dry (you may have to bake the cover for five minutes), rub a cotton swab on one of the chalks or pastels to pick up the color, and gently rub it onto the stamped image (photo 2). Use a different swab for each color.

4 For the back cover, texture the other sheet of clay with interesting objects or rubber stamps. Cut it to the same size as the front cover. Bake them both for 30 minutes, and let them cool.

5 Cut a long strip from your sheet of large paper, 1/2 inch smaller (in height) than the clay covers. Fold the strip of paper back and forth accordion-style (like you're making a paper fan), making it just a little less wide than the book covers (photo 3). If there's a little extra at the end, cut it off. Crease the folds by running your fingernail over each one.

6 To attach the paper to the covers, run the glue stick over one of the end pages, and press the paper firmly to the inside of the clay cover (photo 4). Repeat with the back cover.

7 If you'd like decorative endpapers in your book, cut two pieces of pretty paper a little smaller than the book covers and a little larger than the pages glued into the ends of the book. Glue these decorative paper sheets over the first and last pages (photo 5).

Space Mobile

Intergalactic! Cosmic! Out of this world!

What You Need

- Polymer clay:
  4 ounces glow-in-the-dark
  Small amount of silver
- Star, moon, etc. cookie cutters or templates on page 108
- Rolling tool
- Needle tool
- 6-inch wood or plastic embroidery hoop*
- Lightweight fishing line or black sewing thread
- Tape measure
- Tape
- Glue
- Small "S" hook for hanging mobile**

* Available at craft stores

** Available at home improvement centers

What You Do

1. Roll the glow-in-the-dark clay into a sheet about 1/8 inch thick.

2. Make the celestial objects by cutting out six shapes with the cookie cutters. You can use the templates on page 108 as well. Decorate the shapes with small pieces of silver polymer clay, as shown in photo 1.

3. Poke a small hole in the top of each shape with the needle tool. Bake the shapes for 20 minutes. Glow-in-the-dark clay can sometimes burn easily, so use an aluminum foil tent over the baking tray (see page 21).

4. To make the hanger for the mobile, cut three pieces of fishing line or thread, each about 12 inches long. Tie them onto the hoop so they're spaced evenly around it. Bring the three ends together, and tie a knot (photo 2).

5. Once the shapes are cooled, tape a 2-foot length of fishing line to each one (photo 3). Determine which two shapes are the heaviest, and tie them to the hoop opposite each other. Tie the rest of the shapes onto the hoop at varying heights. Try to space them evenly apart.

6. Put the "S" hook in the loop you made in step 4. Ask an assistant to hold the mobile up in the air. Move the shapes up or down on their strings until the mobile is balanced, and you like the range of heights. When they're where you want them, remove the tape, tie each piece to its string, and snip off the excess. Glue the strings to the embroidery hoop.

Prehistoric Pencil Cup

Get totally Neanderthal with this instant ancient artifact.

What You Need

- Polymer clay:
  4 ounces light tan
  ¼ ounce black
  Tan and black
  jellyroll cane
  (see page 19)
  Red, black, and
  gold triangular bull's-eye
  cane (see pages 19 and 37)

- Jar

- Rolling tool

- Toothpick

- Coarse sandpaper

- Brown or burnt umber
  acrylic paint

- Paper towels

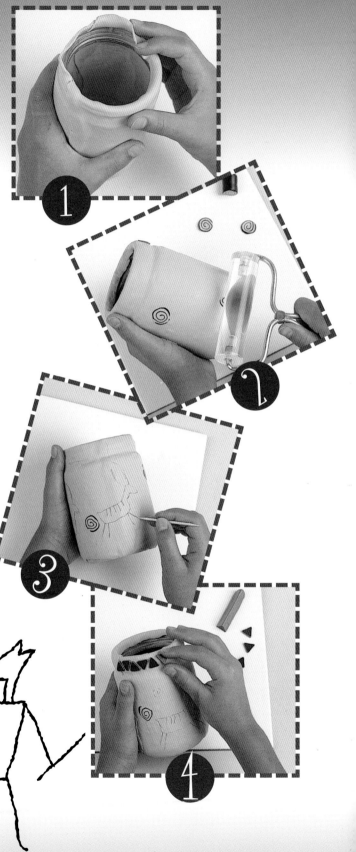

What You Do

1 Find the perfect pencil-cup-sized jar, and wash and dry it thoroughly. Roll out a sheet of light tan clay. Wrap it around the jar, pressing from the middle outward to eliminate any air bubbles. Leave the edges very ragged to enhance that just-excavated look. Be sure to cover the bottom of the jar, too, and wrap the clay just slightly over the lip of the jar (photo 1).

2 Make the jellyroll cane (see page 19), using some of the same tan clay rolled up in black. Cut a few thin slices, lay them onto the jar, and roll them into the background (photo 2).

3 Use the toothpick to etch images into the clay. Hold the jar cupped gently in one hand, and etch with the other. Don't push the toothpick all the way through to the jar;

just scratch the images onto the surface (photo 3). If you make a mistake, smooth the clay with your thumb and start again.

4 Texture the clay with sandpaper just a little in random places. You can also make some nicks and scratches in the clay if you haven't made enough already.

5 Apply some slices of a cane around the rim of the jar (photo 4). (This project uses a triangular bull's-eye cane—see page 37). Bake the clay-covered jar for 30 minutes. Allow it to cool completely.

53

6 With your fingers, spread brown or burnt umber acrylic paint onto the jar, in small sections (photo 5). When you've painted one section, rub the extra paint off with a paper towel (photo 6). Continue until you've painted and wiped the entire surface. If the paint dries before you can wipe it off, wet it with a drop or two of water and rewipe.

Holiday Tin

Turn any plain, old, ordinary candy or cookie tin into a keepsake for a favorite holiday.

1

2

3

4

- Polymer clay:
  2 ounces green
  1 ounce red
  ¼ ounce brown
  ½ ounce white
  Small amounts of
    various other colors
  Slices of purchased or
    handmade small, simple
    canes (see page 19)

- Clean candy tin

- Rolling tool

- Wax paper

- Butter knife

- Template on page 108

- Glitter (optional)

- Small, star-shaped
  cookie cutter

1 Roll out a sheet of green clay about ⅛ inch thick and big enough to cover the bottom of the tin. Lay it onto a piece of wax paper.

2 Pick up the wax paper, and with the tin bottom-side up, lay the clay onto the bottom of the tin. Work out the air bubbles by pressing the wax paper from one edge of the tin to the other (photo 1).

3 Turn the tin right-side up, and set it onto your work surface. With the knife, carefully trim the excess clay from the bottom (photo 2). Peel off the wax paper.

4 Roll out a thin ribbon of green clay, and trim one of the long edges straight. Starting at the center between the hinges of the tin, lay the ribbon around the entire circumference of the bottom half of the tin (photo 3).

5 Carefully trim off the excess clay at the bottom edge. Be sure to trim a little more clay off around the hinges so the top will be able to open easily. Smooth all seams with your fingertip. Bake for 10 minutes.

6 When the tin has cooled completely, repeat all of the above steps to cover the top of the tin with red clay.

7 Roll a sheet of white clay for the snow. Lay this onto the bottom section of the top of the tin, wrapping it around the edges and trimming off the excess (photo 4).

8 For the tree trunk, roll a small piece of brown clay into a log, and taper one end to a blunt point. Place the trunk onto the upper part of the snow, centered on the lid (photo 5).

9 Cut a tree shape from a thin sheet of green clay (can use the template on page 108). If you want, mix some glitter into the green clay when you condition it. Lay the tree onto the lid, making sure to cover the tree trunk's top edge.

10 Decorate the tree with very thin snakes of clay for a garland. Place slices from tiny canes and tiny balls of colored clay for ornaments. Top the tree with a star cut from the yellow clay (photo 6). Add presents under the tree if you want. Bake your finished tin for 30 minutes.

57

Beetlemania

Make 'em, name 'em, and give 'em a home on your refrigerator, school locker, desk, or any other metallic surface. Don't worry; they're not picky.

What You Need

- ▸ Polymer clay:
  Fun colors of scrap clay
  ¼ ounce black
- ▸ Polymer clay cutting blade
- ▸ Rolling tool
- ▸ 1½-inch circle cookie cutter
- ▸ Circle cutters in various sizes
- ▸ Needle tool
- ▸ Thin craft wire in various colors
- ▸ Wire cutters
- ▸ Magnet
- ▸ Cyanoacrylate glue

1 (Steps 1 through 6 show you how to create a cool "mirror technique." It's fun, but you can skip it if you wish, and simply create any kind of dome shape for your bug.) Marble two colors of scrap clay (see page 17) (photo 1).

2 Push the ends of the snake toward each other, making it fatter and about 1 ½ inches long. Flatten this to make it a thick rectangle.

3 With the blade, slice through the center of the rectangle, and carefully pull the halves apart. The halves will be mirror images of each other (photo 2).

4 Lay the halves next to each other, matching up the pattern in the center. With your roller, gently flatten to a ⅛-inch thickness to unite the pieces.

5 Cut a circle from this piece using the 1 ½-inch circle cutter, making sure the center of the mirror image is in the center of the circle (photo 3). Set it aside.

6 Roll a small ball of scrap clay about ½ inch in diameter. With the palm of your hand, flatten it slightly to form a dome (photo 4). Drape the mirror image circle on top of the dome, and press around the edges to cover it (photo 5).

60

7 Use the needle tool to make a straight indentation following the center line of the mirror image. This divides the bug body in half visually.

8 Roll out a small thin sheet of clay in a color that looks nice with your bug body. Cut a circle from it. Then cut this circle in half. These half-circles are the wings. Place the wings onto the bug body, touching where the head will be and opening over the sides (photo 6).

9 Roll a ball of black clay for the head, and press it to the bug where the wings connect (photo 7).

10 For the antennae, wrap some colored wire around the needle tool many times. Slide it off, cut it in half with the wire cutters, and stretch it out a little bit. Screw a piece of wire into the bug's head on both sides (photo 8). You can also twist beads onto

the wire for the ends of the antennae. Or have many different-sized wings stacked on top of each other. For further decoration, add tiny balls of clay or tiny cane slices to the wings. Bake your bug for 30 minutes, and when cool, glue the magnet to the bottom.

Plant Critters

These little guys have a point. And that point is perfect for sticking into dirt. Your houseplants will welcome the company.

- Polymer clay:
  1+ ounces of a color of
  your choice*
  Less than ¼ ounce of
  2 to 3 other colors*

- Various sculpting tools:
  golf tee, toothpick, small
  paintbrush (see page 12)

- Polymer clay cutting
  blade

* Quantities needed for
  one critter

What You Do

1 Roll the main color of clay into a log about 4 to 5 inches long. Taper one end into a blunt point that's not too thin so that it can't be pushed into the soil (photo 1).

2 On the wide end of the clay log, use the golf tee (or the pointy end of a small paintbrush) to make indentations for the eyes.

3 To make the eyes, roll a contrasting color of clay into a ball a little bigger than a pea. Cut it in half with the cutting tool. Then roll each of the halves into a ball. This will give you eyes that are the same size. Place these into the eye sockets, and press them in gently so they stay in place (photo 2).

4 For the irises, roll a really tiny piece of clay into a piece about the size of a grain of rice. Cut it exactly in half. Roll each of these into a teeny, tiny ball between your fingertips, and place them on the eyeballs (photo 3). You can center them exactly or make them look off to one side or in different directions.

5 For eyelids, roll a piece of clay that's the same color as the body into a thin sheet. Cut two strips about 1/2 inch wide and 3/4 inch long. Set them in place over the eyes. Gently press them into place with the golf tee or pointy paintbrush end. Blend the seams between the lids and the body, and use your fingers to smooth the clay. You can create eyelashes by making indentations with the toothpick (photo 4).

6 Choose another color of clay for the nose, and pinch off a small ball the size of a pea. Roll it into a short cone shape and set it aside.

7 Use the golf tee to make a dot where you want the nose. Insert the point a tiny bit, and move it in a circle to make an indentation that's similar in size and width to the pointed end of the nose cone (photo 5). Pick up the nose, and set it into the indentation. Press gently so it sticks. You can reshape the nose a little bit, and use the end of the golf tee to make nostrils.

8 Create a round mouth with the pen. Press the point into the clay and wiggle it back and forth to make an "O" shape (photo 6). Or use the craft knife to cut partway into the clay below the nose, and then gently pull the top and bottom away from each other.

9 If you want to add antennae, ears, or a mohawk, curl a piece of wire or make a piece of clay the appropriate shape, and set it in place. Blend any seams with a sculpting tool, then smooth them with your finger. Create a body gesture by making a gentle bend in the body or leaning the head to one side (photo 7). Bake on a wadded-up paper towel for at least 30 minutes.

10 Make several of these, and put them into the family's houseplants, and see how long it takes family members to notice.

5

6

7

65

Tic-Tac-Toe

Once you've mastered making the tic-tac-toe pieces and board, try checkers, and if you're really adventurous, create a totally unique, out-of-this-world chess set.

What You Need

- Polymer clay:
  8 ounces black
  4 ounces white
- Rolling tool
- 6 x 6-inch smooth glazed ceramic tile
- Craft knife
- Ruler
- Needle tool or pencil
- 1 ½-inch- and 1-inch-diameter circle cutters

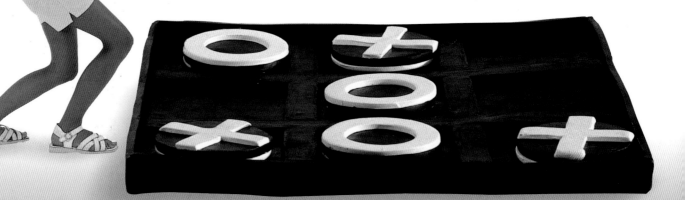

What You Do

1 For the game board, roll the black polymer clay into a large sheet about ⅛ inch thick and a little bigger than the tile. Completely cover the tile with the sheet (photo 1). Release air bubbles with the rolling tool—rolling from the center out to the edges. With the craft knife, trim the edges even with the edges of the tile.

2 Roll the rest of the black clay into a sheet as long as the tile. With the ruler as a guide, use the craft knife to cut eight strips each about ¼ inch wide (photo 2). These are the grid lines for the board.

3 Use the ruler and craft knife to mark 2-inch intervals on the game board along the edges (photo 3). These will help you place the grid lines.

4 Center one of the black strips over the 2-inch mark, and carefully lay it across to the mark on the other side of the base. Repeat with another strip, at the other 2-inch mark on that edge (photo 4). Gently but firmly press these into place.

5 Place the grid lines in the other direction now, but don't press them into place yet. Use the craft knife to cut and remove the pieces of clay from the top strips where they overlap the bottom ones (see photo 5 on page 68). Now you can press them into place. Press the seams together, and smooth them with your fingertips (see photo 6 on page 68). Trim the edges.

6 Use the remaining four strips along the edges of the game board to create walls for the sides (photo 7).

7 For the game pieces, roll black and white clay into ⅛-inch-thick sheets. Cut 18 circles from the sheets with a 1 ½-inch circle cutter (nine white, nine black). Make the white circles into "O"s by cutting out the centers with a smaller, 1-inch-diameter circle cutter (photo 8). Place the white "O"s onto the black circles.

8 For the "X"s, cut thin strips from the sheet of white clay. Turn all the game pieces upside down, and apply one strip of white across the center of each. Apply the other strip over the top of the first one, crossing it to make an "X" (photo 9). Trim where the strips overlap, and smooth the seams.

9 Trim the excess white clay from the "X"s from the game piece sides. Bake the board and game pieces for 30 minutes. When the game board is cool, you can pop it off the tile.

Big Fat Pen

The only thing better than a beautiful pen is a beautiful FAT pen. If this pen is too fat for you, use a thinner sheet of clay in step 1.

Karla

What You Need

▸ Polymer clay:
  4 ounces of any color
  Your choice of a hand-
  made or purchased
  cane (see page 19)

▸ Pen with a white plas-
  tic or gray rubber barrel*

▸ Rolling tool

▸ Polymer clay cutting
  blade

▸ Piece of paper

▸ Cornstarch or talcum
  powder

* Clear plastic pens will melt!

What You Do

1 Remove the ink catridge from the pen, and set aside. Roll the clay into a thick 1/4-inch sheet. Cut one edge straight, and place the pen barrel along this edge. Cut the clay as long as the pen, leaving a little extra at the top end. Roll the sheet of clay around the pen, and trim the sheet so that it covers the pen but doesn't overlap (photo 1).

2 Pinch the top closed. Gently and slowly roll the pen on your work surface to make sure the clay is smooth and sticking to the pen really well (photo 2). If any air bubbles show up, slice them open with the cutting tool and reseal the clay.

3 Place cane slices on the pen (photo 3). When you've covered the pen, roll it again to press the slices in and even them out. Trim away any clay that has been pushed beyond the edge of the barrel on the end of the pen where you'll need to reinsert the ink cartridge later.

4 Fold a piece of paper into an accordion shape, place the pen on one of the folds, and bake for 30 minutes (photo 4).

5 Roll the rest of your solid color of polymer clay into a ball for the holder. Cover it with cane slices to match the pen, and roll it in the palms of your hands until the slices are all well-adhered to the clay.

6 Press down from the top to flatten the bottom of the ball, but leave the top rounded (photo 5).

7 When the pen has cooled off, put the ink cartridge back in. Then lightly dust some cornstarch or talcum powder onto the pen tip. Decide where you want the pen to stick into the holder—at a slight angle just to the side of the center works nicely—and press the pen in at this point. Push it in as deeply as you can without going all the way through to the bottom (photo 6). Twist the pen in your fingers a bit so the hole is nice and round, but don't move it around so much that you make the hole wider than the pen.

8 Remove the pen from the holder, clean off any excess cornstarch on the pen with a paper towel, and bake the holder for 40 minutes.

Framed!

W hy settle for a boring picture frame when, with a little polymer clay and some gel pens, you can create a frame that's a masterpiece all by itself?

What You Need

- Polymer clay: 2 ounces black
- Rolling tool
- 4 x 6-inch acrylic picture frame
- Rubber stamps*
- Paper towels
- Craft knife
- Assorted gel pens
- Scissors
- Craft glue

* All rubber-stamped images used here are by Impression-Obsession.

What You Do

1 Roll out a large sheet of the black clay about ⅛ inch thick. The sheet should be larger than the frame.

2 Use the rubber stamps to decorate the sheet (photo 1). Dampen the stamp each time you're going to use it by pressing it onto a wet paper towel before stamping it onto the clay.

3 Gently place the acrylic frame face-down on the clay sheet. Trim the excess clay at the bottom edge of the frame with the craft knife so the edge of the sheet is even with the frame.

4 To make the shape for your frame, use the craft knife to cut the clay around the outside of the acrylic frame (photo 2). You can use a gently curved shape like in the photo or maybe jagged edges like monster teeth. After you've cut the outer shape, remove the acrylic frame, and set it aside. Remove the excess clay from the outside of the shape you designed.

5 Cut a piece of scrap paper to the size and shape you want for the frame opening (where the photograph will go). Center it on the clay, and cut the clay around the paper (photo 3). Remove the excess clay.

6 Smooth any edges that need it, and bake for 20 minutes.

7 When the frame has finished baking, remove it from the oven while it's still warm, and put it on a flat surface. Set your heaviest science book on top of it so it remains flat as it cools. A math book will also work.

8 When the frame has cooled completely (it should take about 30 minutes), use gel pens to color the stamped areas of the frame. Not all gel pens show up on dark clay, so experiment to see which ones give you the best results.

9 After you've colored the frame with the gel pens, put the frame back in the oven at about 250°F for 10 to 15 minutes. This sets the gel inks so they won't rub off. When it's cooled off again, use the craft glue to attach the clay to the acrylic frame (photo 4).

73

Marbled Pendant

I t's stylish, chic, avant-garde! To further impress friends, create matching earrings.

What You Need

- Polymer clay:
  ½ ounce each of black and white
  Small amounts of purple and lime green
- Rolling tool
- Needle tool, bamboo skewer, or toothpick
- Small circle cookie cutter
- Polymer clay cutting blade
- Jar lid or other flat object
- 2-inch head pin*
- Round-nose and flat-nose pliers
- Wire cutters
- 3 feet of 1 mm black rubber or leather cord

* Can be found in bead and craft stores

1 Roll two pea-sized balls of lime green clay, and set them aside. Roll the white polymer clay into a log about 1 inch high and 2 inches long. Roll the purple, lime green, and part of the black clay into skinny snakes, and lay them lengthwise on the white log (photo 1). Some of the white should still show between the colored snakes.

2 Press the snakes into the white log. Then roll the log with light pressure to flatten the colored snakes into the white log (photo 2).

3 Start twisting the log so the snake colors spiral around the log. Try to keep the log the same length as you twist, and roll it on your work surface after every few twists to keep it smooth. Keep twisting and rolling until the colors look like skinny stripes around the log (photo 3).

1

2

3

4

75

4 Set the log on your work surface, and flatten it until you have a 1/8-inch-thick sheet (see photo 4 on page 75).

5 Drag the tip of the needle tool, toothpick, or bamboo skewer up and down across the stripes to create the marbled pattern (photo 5). Use enough pressure to pull the stripes through one another.

6 Flatten the raised burrs with the rolling tool. Find areas of the pattern that turned out really nicely, and cut out two circles with the cookie cutter (photo 6).

7 Roll the black clay into a smooth ball. Use the jar lid to press it into a thick, flat disk that's slightly larger than the marbled circles (photo 7). Center a marbled circle on each side of the black disk, putting the stripes in the same direc-tion on both sides. Press gently to stick the pieces of clay together, but not so hard that you distort them.

8 Use the needle tool to make a hole side-to-side through the center of the disk. Press the pea-sized balls of lime green clay onto the holes, and use the needle tool to poke through the green clay and into the black disk (photo 8).

9 Bake the pendant for 30 minutes. When cool, insert the head pin through the hole. Loop the end of the head pin around the widest part of the pliers tips, and curl the free end of the head pin around the bottom of the loop with the flat-nose pliers. Snip off the extra eye pin with the wire cutters. Thread and knot the rubber or leather cord through the pin.

Tick Tock Clock

H ere's a timepiece that tells time and looks great!

What You Need

- Polymer clay:
  2 ounces magenta
  ½ ounce each
    of yellow, orange,
    turquoise, green, and
    fuchsia

- Wooden clock base*

- Heat-resistant PVA
  glue

- Rolling tool

- Wax paper

- Craft knife

- Sandpaper

- Texturing tools (see
  page 12)

- Small shape cutters

- Clock face template on
  page 108

- Permanent marker

- Black, gold, and glow-in-
  the-dark fabric paints in
  squeeze bottles

- Clockworks and clock
  hands*

- Battery

* Available at craft
  stores

1 Cover the wooden clock base with a thin coat of glue, and let it dry. This will allow the clay to stick to the surface better. Roll out a sheet of magenta polymer clay about ⅛ inch thick and a little larger than the face of the clock.

2 Gently place the magenta clay onto the wooden clock face without pressing down. Starting at the center and working outward, smooth the clay onto the wooden base with the brayer or your fingers (photo 1). If it's sticky, and you're leaving marks, put a piece of wax paper on top of the clay first. Make sure the clay makes complete contact with the wood.

3 Wrap the edges of the clay around the edges of the clock face. Trim away any excess clay from the back of the clock (photo 2). Cut out and remove the clay that's covering the hole in the center of the clock. Texture the clock face with the sandpaper. Set the clock aside.

4 Roll out sheets of various colors of clay. Texture each of the sheets with different tools, and cut out assorted shapes with the shapes cutters (photo 3). (You can also cut shapes freehand, if you wish.)

5 Press the shapes very gently into place with a piece of wax paper so you don't get fingerprints on the clay. When you absolutely LOVE the clock you've assembled, bake it for 30 minutes.

6 When the clock is baked and cooled, center the clock template on page 108 over the hole in the center of the clock, making sure one line goes straight up and down, for 12 and 6 (photo 4). Use the markings as a guide, and make a tiny dot on the clock face with the marker for each number.

7 Remove the paper template, and place a dot of glow-in-the-dark fabric paint on each of the marker dots (photo 5). Use the other colors of fabric paint to add lines and dots and squiggles around or on the textured clay shapes. If you want, decorate the clock hands with the fabric paints as well. Let the clock dry overnight.

8 Assemble the clock according to the clockworks manufacturer's instructions, and add a battery.

Fine Feathered Friends

Create a whole flock of these far-out feathered friends, and let them hang out in your nest.

What You Need

- ▸ Polymer clay:
  1 ounce of your favorite color
  Small amounts (pinches) of other colors
  A few slices from small canes (see page 19)

- ▸ Feathers

- ▸ Brightly colored craft wire

- ▸ Wire cutters

- ▸ Polymer clay cutting blade

- ▸ Toothpick

- ▸ Polyester batting or piece of cotton cloth

- ▸ Cyanoacrylate glue

- ▸ 12 inches of thread in any color

What You Do

1 Divide the ounce of polymer clay into two pieces—one should be about three times larger than the other. Roll both pieces into balls, and set the smaller one aside for the bird's head.

2 Taper the larger ball by rolling it back and forth on your work surface, putting pressure just on one side. Taper it until it's as long as you want the bird's body to be. The pointy end will be the tail.

82

3 Attach the head to the body by pressing it onto the wider end of the large piece. Use enough pressure to make it stick, but not so much that you distort the clay. Then, shape the body a little by curving the pointy end upward (photo 1).

4 Cut a piece of wire about ½ inch long, and bend it into a "U" shape with legs. Insert this into the top of the body, behind the head (photo 2). This is what the bird will hang from. Squeeze the clay closed, and smooth over the insertion points.

5 Decorate! Add cane slices to the head, the breast, the tail, the sides (photo 3). Create teeny, tiny balls, flatten them onto the body, and use coiled wire for the crest if you want. Roll a pointy little beak, and press it onto the head. Be sure to add eyes.

6 Make the holes for the wings on the sides of the body by inserting the toothpick and angling it slightly toward the top (photo 4). If you poke the holes straight in, the wings will stick straight out. Oh, don't forget to make a hole on the pointy end of the bird's rear end for his tail feather.

7 Set the bird on the piece of polyester batting or bunched-up cotton cloth on a baking sheet (photo 5). Bake it for 30 minutes. When the bird is cool, insert the feathers to make sure they fit properly. Pull them out, and trim them to the length you want. Put a tiny dab of glue on the end of each feather, and put it into place. Pass the thread through the hanging wire, and knot it.

Bodacious Bauble Bowl

Y our trinkets are tired of ending up on the floor or stuck in the washing machine with your jeans. They want respect. Build this bowl for them.

What You Do

1 Turn the cereal bowl upside down. You'll build your clay bowl on the outside of the oven-safe bowl. Start with a cane slice about ⅛ inch thick. Place it on the center of the bottom of the bowl. Roll a piece of clay in a coordinating color into a thin, short snake, and surround the cane slice with it (photo 1).

2 Work your way outward by adding more cane slices. You can work randomly or symmetrically.

3 You can roll a piece of clay into a small ball (smaller than a pea), flatten it, and place it in between any cane slices that have gaps between them (photo 2).

4 Continue working outward from the center, placing cane slices or small pieces of flattened solid colors of clay. Press the slices and clay gently but firmly against the

What You Need

▸ Polymer clay:
Several purchased or handmade canes in various colors and shapes (see page 19)
¼ ounce each of various colors

▸ Small, oven-safe cereal bowl

▸ Polymer clay cutting blade

▸ Wax paper

▸ Rolling tool

pieces already in place. You can press the seams lightly with your finger, but don't rub them or the colors may smear.

5 Continue adding clay until you like how the bowl looks. Be sure you've built it large enough to extend down the sloped sides of the bowl slightly. Lay a piece of wax paper over the clay on the bowl, and gently smooth over the bowl with your fingers or the rolling tool (see photo 3 on page 85).

6 Roll three short cylinders of clay (your choice of colors) for legs. Place these on the bottom of the bowl, spaced evenly apart (see photo 4 on page 85). You can add a cane slice to the bottom of each leg if you want.

7 Turn the bowl over and place it, legs down, onto a piece of wax paper. If you need to, press lightly over one leg to even out how it stands.

8 Turn the bowl over again, and peel away the wax paper from the bottoms of the legs. Bake it right on the cereal bowl upside down, for 30 minutes. When it has cooled completely, pull gently, working around the edge of the polymer clay bowl, until it releases from the cereal bowl. Use a toothpick if it's stuck (photo 5). The inside will be smooth and shiny from where it was in contact with the cereal bowl. It's now the perfect place for your trinkets and treasures.

Hold the Pickles

Create a medium-rare fashion statement—fast food never looked so good!

87

1 These instructions are for the pendant. Buns first. Roll some light tan clay into two balls—one the size of a marble and the other a bit larger. Flatten the balls slightly with your fingers, making the smaller one flat on both top and bottom, and leaving the larger ball slightly domed on the top (photo 1).

2 Lettuce next. Flatten a pea-sized ball of green clay onto wax paper—make it as thin as possible. Slide the edge of the cutting blade under the clay to pick it up from the wax paper. Tear it into a piece the right size for your bun, and place it on the bottom (flatter) half of the bun (photo 2).

3 Now the burger. Roll brown clay into a ball the size of a marble. Flatten it slightly and texture it gently (see page 12) with the sandpaper (photo 3). Place the burger on top of the lettuce.

What You Need

- Polymer clay: Approximately ¼ ounce each of brown, light brown (or tan), green, red, yellow, purple, white, and translucent
- Polymer clay cutting blade
- Rolling tool
- Wax paper
- Sandpaper
- Toothpick
- Brown chalk (optional)
- Cord for stringing pendant (approximately 24 inches long)
- 2 pieces of plastic-coated wire, 1 inch long each
- Earring hooks
- Cyanoacrylate glue

1

2

3

4

4 It's a cheeseburger, of course! Mix a really teeny, tiny amount of red clay into a small amount of yellow clay to make an orangey-yellow. Flatten this into a small, thin sheet. Use the blade to cut a square piece of cheese, and set it in place. Very gently push the corners down over the burger, so the cheese appears to be melted (photo 4).

5 Of course we need some tomatoes. Roll a small amount of red into a short, thin log. Slice a few pieces from it, and place them onto the cheese.

6 Onions! Mix white and purple to get a pale purple. Roll this into a flat sheet. Roll a piece of translucent clay into a flat sheet the same size, place it onto the pale purple clay, and roll a jellyroll cane (see page 19). Cut a few slices, and place them on the top of the burger (photo 5).

7 Use the toothpick to press an indentation across the top of the onions. Roll the toothpick to smooth the indentation (photo 6). This will be for the cord of your pendant.

8 Finally, gently press the top of the bun onto your delicious-looking creation. If you want your bun to look toasted, scrape some brown chalk onto a piece of paper. Dab your finger into it, tap off the excess, and gently rub it onto the top of the bun.

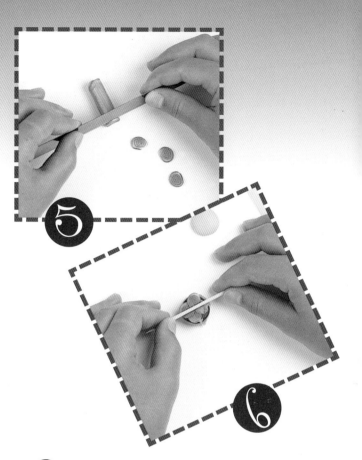

9 Bake for 30 minutes. When it's cool, thread the cord through the hole under the top of the bun.

10 For the earrings, follow the instructions above, but make the pieces smaller. Skip step 7. Instead, push a small loop of wire carefully into the top of each bun after step 8, and attach earring hooks.

spirit Doll

A spirit doll can be an expression of who you are right now, your idea of what you want to be, or simply a collection of your favorite shapes, colors, textures, and embedded objects. What will yours look like?

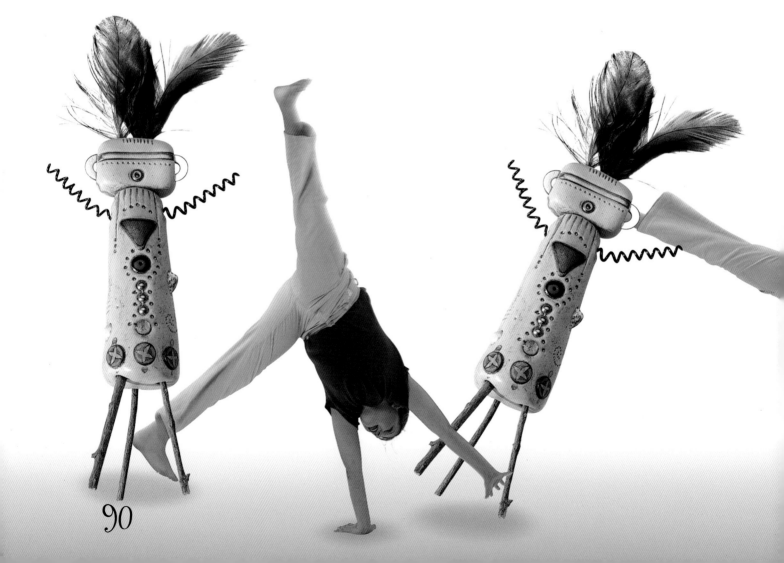

What You Need

- Polymer clay:
  1 ½ ounces tan or ecru
  Cane slices (see page 19)
- 3 thin sticks
- Heat-resistant PVA glue
- Polymer clay cutting blade
- Craft knife
- Miscellaneous found objects such as beads or small shells
- Toothpick
- Craft wire
- Wire cutters
- Needle tool
- Polyester batting or a bunched-up cotton rag
- Cyanoacrylate glue
- Metal washers or other objects
- Metallic gold paint (or color of your choice)
- Paper towels
- Feathers

What You Do

1 Coat about 1 inch of one end of each stick (the legs) with a thin layer of glue. This will help the sticks stay in the clay. Set these aside to dry.

2 For the body, lop off about one quarter of your polymer clay for the head, and set it aside. Roll the rest into a short, fat tube about as long as your thumb. Taper one end just a little by putting a bit of pressure on that end as you roll the log (photo 1).

3 Press each end of the log onto your work surface so both ends of the log are flat (photo 2).

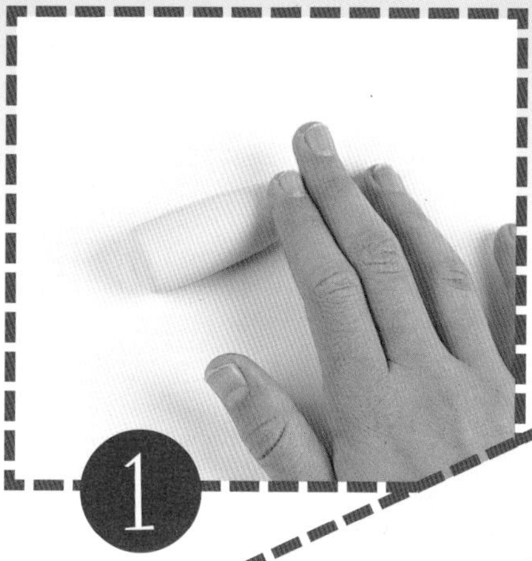

1

2

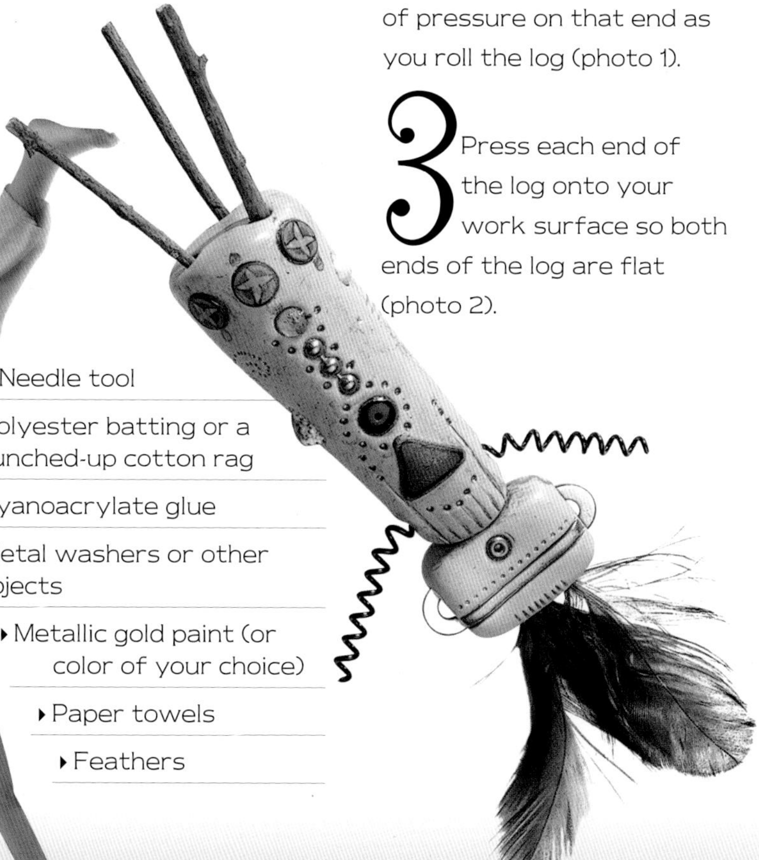

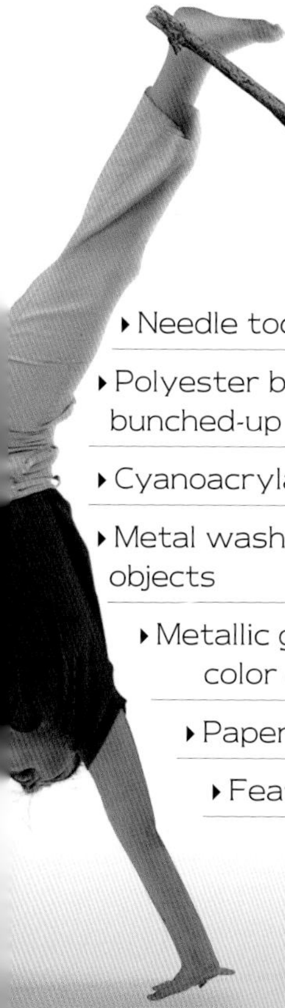

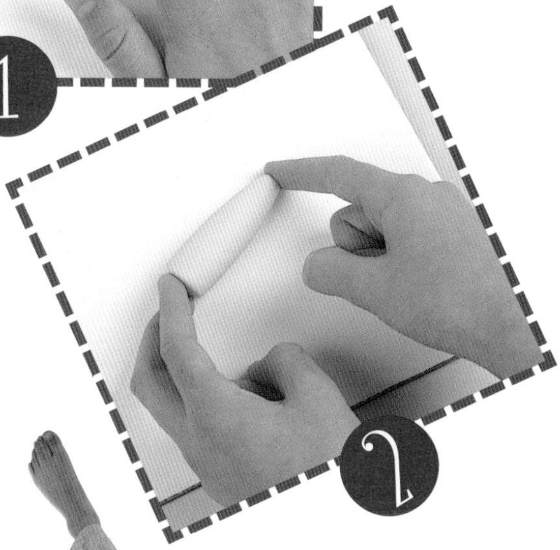

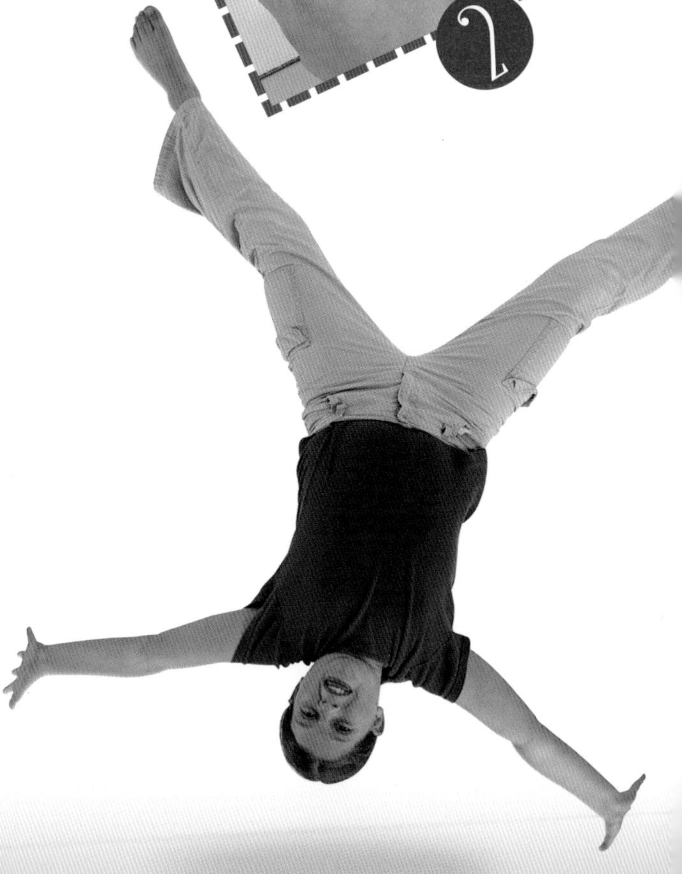

4 Are those legs dry yet? If so, insert them into the wide end of the tapered log. Push them in slowly, and make sure each is pointing slightly outward. Trim the legs until the doll stands evenly.

5 Set the body on its side and very, very carefully, roll it just enough to tighten the clay around the leg holes (photo 3).

6 Now's the time to let the spirit of the doll speak to you and tell you that it wants its body lovingly decorated with shells, cane slices, or metal things. If she ain't talking, you can decide for yourself. Make an indentation for each non-clay object you want to add (photo 4), place a tiny drop of glue in the indentation, and press the shell, bead, or whatever into place. Keep adding stuff until you're happy.

7 Use the toothpick to make little dots and other decorations. Hold the toothpick perpendicular to the body, and press it in slightly to make lines (photo 5).

8 For the arms, curl a piece of wire tightly around the needle tool (photo 6). Pull it off, and stretch it out a bit. Cut it in half with the wire cutters, and screw an arm into each side of the body (photo 7).

9 For the head, roll the remaining polymer clay into a ball, form it into a squarish shape with your fingers, and flatten it slightly. Add some beads or other objects (photo 8), as well as some decorative marks with the toothpick. Also, make holes in the top of the head (one for each feather you want to add).

10 Set the head on the body, and gently press it into place. Set the entire doll on its side on a piece of polyester batting or a bunched-up cotton rag, and bake for 30 to 40 minutes.

11 When the doll is completely baked and cool, check for any loose pieces. If anything comes off, glue it back into place with some cyanoacrylate glue.

12 To highlight the texture, squirt some metallic gold paint onto it, and rub it in every nook and cranny with a finger (photo 9). Quickly wipe the excess paint off with a paper towel.

13 When the paint's completely dry, choose some feathers for headgear. Snip them to the length you want, dot a bit of glue onto the end of each, and set them into place.

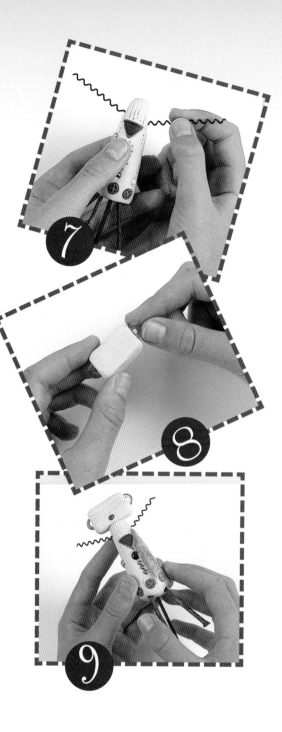

93

Locker Mirror

Yes, yes, you're the fairest one of all. Now get to class.

What You Need

- ▸ Polymer clay:
  4 ounces dark blue
  (depends on the size of
  your mirror)
- ▸ Rolling tool
- ▸ Small mirror (from a
  craft store)
- ▸ Wax paper
- ▸ Talcum powder or corn
  starch
- ▸ Rubber stamps
- ▸ Craft knife
- ▸ White acrylic paint
- ▸ Paper towels
- ▸ Rubbing alcohol
- ▸ 2 to 4 strong magnets
- ▸ Cyanoacrylate glue

What You Do

1 Roll a sheet of clay that's larger than the mirror by at least an inch in every direction, and that's as thick as the mirror. Place it on a piece of wax paper.

2 With a fingertip, lightly dust the clay with powder or cornstarch. Press the rubber stamps into the clay. Use a variety of images if you want a collage. You'll be removing the center of the clay for the mirror and trimming the outer edges, so concentrate your artistic efforts accordingly.

3 When you're finished decorating, place the mirror in the middle of the sheet. Use the craft knife to cut the clay around the mirror (photo 1). Remove the mirror and the piece of clay under it. Set the clay aside, and put the mirror in the hole you just made.

4 To create the back of the mirror frame, cover the mirror and clay frame with another piece of wax paper, and flip the whole thing over. Remove the wax paper.

5 Roll the extra clay into another slab as thick as the first one. Place this over the back of the mirror and

95

frame. Press it into place, but don't distort the stamped images on the other side by pressing too hard.

6 Cover with a sheet of wax paper, and flip the whole thing over once again. Remove the top piece of wax paper, and use the craft knife to trim the frame to the size and shape you want (photo 2).

7 If you'd like to add some embellishments, now's the time. The frame in the photograph has some thin pieces of a striped cane (see page 19) just under the bottom of the mirror.

8 Peel the wax paper from the back of the frame, and bake for 30 minutes. When the frame has cooled completely, remove the mirror by flexing the frame very gently until they sepa-

rate (photo 3). Set the mirror aside.

9 To highlight the stamped images, rub some acrylic paint into the clay with your finger. Make sure to push it into all the indentations you made with the stamps (photo 4). As soon as you rub the paint on, immediately wipe it off with a paper towel. You can add more paint if you need to or remove some more with a damp paper towel (photo 5).

10 Wipe the back of the mirror and frame with a bit of rubbing alcohol on a paper towel or cotton ball. Also wipe out the recess where the mirror will be glued in. The alcohol removes any oils that might keep the glue from doing its thing. Glue the mirror into place, and then glue the magnets onto the back. Use at least two magnets.

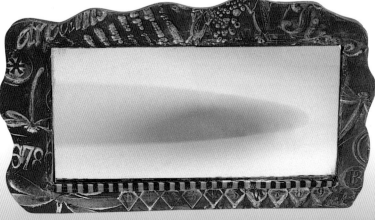

Flower Power Vase

T he flowers on the outside of this vase will stick around a lot longer than the ones inside.

What You Need

- Polymer clay:
  1 ounce each of 2 shades of green
  1 ounce each of 2 shades of blue
  ½ ounce yellow
- Clean glass vase or jar
- Polymer clay cutting blade
- Golf tee
- Toothpick

①

②

③

What You Do

1 Roll the green clays into two long snakes, not quite as thick around as your pinky. Press down along one side of each green snake to create a teardrop shape (photo 1).

2 Use the cutting blade to cut a bajillion slices from these snakes. Okay, not a bajillion, but a lot. Each slice is a leaf, so of course the more leaves you want, the more slices you need. If the clay starts to squish too much to one side, flip over the snakes and cut from the other side.

3 Place a clay leaf on the lower portion of the vase. If you touch a clay leaf with your fingertip, it will stick to your finger. Then you can place it on the vase and kind of roll your finger off; the leaf should stick to the glass (photo 2).

4 Repeat step 3 a bajillion times. (That's one for each leaf.) Place each leaf on the glass, pointing upward or slightly to one side. Make sure each leaf is touching other leaves, but also make sure to leave some blank spaces between the leaves for the flowers (photo 3).

5 Cover the lower part of the vase with leaves, mixing the different shades of green randomly. Your fingerprints add interesting texture to the leaves, and you can poke some of them a little with the end of the golf tee to add detail. Set the leafy vase aside.

98

6 Now for the flowers. Roll the blue clays into snakes thinner than your pinky. Each round slice from these snakes will be a flower petal. The flowers on the vase in the photo each have five petals, but you can make yours with three, four, six—whatever you want.

7 Slice a whole lotta slices from the blue snakes. Pick up a slice with your finger and set it onto the vase where there's a blank spot but where the petal will touch a leaf or two. Release the petal onto the vase. Use the golf tee to make an indentation in the petal, near the center of the flower. Apply all the petals for the flower, and then continue making blue flowers all over the vase (photo 4).

8 Roll the yellow clay into a skinny snake, and cut one slice for each flower. Pick up each slice with the toothpick, and set it into the dent in the center of each flower. Poke the toothpick into the yellow clay in several places to give it some texture and to make sure that the centers are stuck to the flowers (photo 5).

9 When you've created a floral masterpiece, set the vase in a cold oven and bring the temperature up to the temperature recommended for that brand of clay. Bake for 30 to 40 minutes.

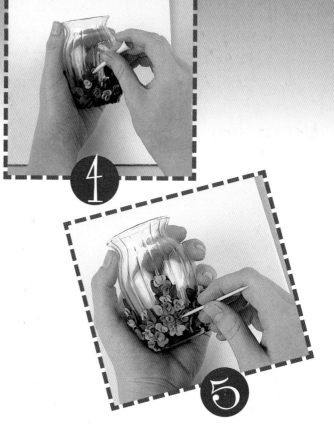

Forget-You-Not Bracelet

I f you ever forget your name, this beautiful bracelet will be right there to remind you. If your name is Delphinium, consider making a necklace instead.

- Polymer clay:
  3 ounces white
  1 ounce each of purple,
  yellow, and green
- Polymer clay cutting blade
- Craft knife
- Rolling tool
- Old credit card or other thin piece of plastic
- Ruler
- Needle tool
- Rubber-stamp alphabet and ink pad
- Assorted beads
- Clear elastic cord
- Cyanoacrylate glue
- Scissors

What You Do

1 Roll about two-thirds of the white clay into a log approximately 4 inches long and half as thick as your index finger. Set it aside.

2 Flatten the yellow, purple, and green clay into thin sheets. Make three sheets the same size with some of the remaining white clay. They don't need to be precisely the same thickness. With the polymer clay cutting blade, trim all the sheets as wide as the log is long—about 4 inches.

3 Stack the sheets in the following order: yellow, white, purple, white, green, white. Press the sheets together carefully to avoid trapping air between the layers (photo 1).

4 Cut the stack in half with the cutting tool, and put one half on top of the other. You've now made a striped cane that will become part of another cane. Use the rolling tool to flatten the new stack to approximately 1/8 inch thick (photo 2). Trim it so the edges are crisp, even, and as wide as the log.

5 Now wrap this layered sheet around the white log creating a bull's-eye cane (see page 19). Trim the edges where they meet with the craft knife, and smooth the seam.

6 To make the cane look like a flower with petals, indent it from the outside by pressing the credit card lengthwise into the cane (photo 3). You don't want to press more than one-third of the way through. Rotate the cane a little, and repeat until you've made six or eight indentations with the card along the length of the cane.

7 Roll the cane gently on the work surface to "seal up" the cuts you made, so that the cane appears fairly smooth again. The indentations have made a petal-like effect that you'll see when you slice the cane.

8 Roll out another thin sheet of any leftover white clay. Wrap the cane with this sheet, trimming the edges and smoothing the seam as you did before (photo 4).

9 Carefully cut the cane into slices each about ¼ inch thick. Pierce holes with the needle tool in each slice, from side to side, to create beads.

10 Place the number of beads required for your bracelet in a row, making sure that all the holes are side-to-side.

11 Ink the alphabet letter stamps you need, and gently stamp each letter onto a bead (photo 5). Don't press into the clay—you just want the ink to transfer from the stamp to the surface of the clay.

12 Bake for 30 minutes. When the beads are cool, string them onto the elastic. Use other beads as spacers and to complete the design. When the bracelet is the right length, tie the elastic ends into a double knot. Add a drop of cyanoacrylate glue to the knot. Allow the glue to dry before trimming the ends.

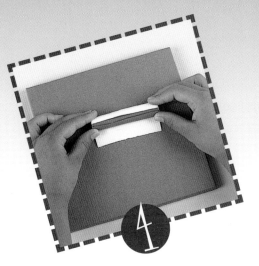

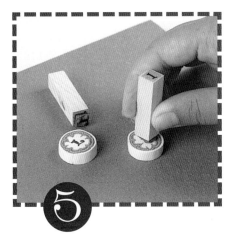

Computer Wizard

This little guy will cast his spell and protect you from lost files and sudden crashes. He can't, however, save you from your homework.

What You Do

1 First you'll make and bake the head and body of this wizard, and then you'll dress him. For his eyes, roll two tiny pieces of black clay into balls the size of a head of a pin. Bake them for 10 minutes and set them aside.

2 For the head, roll a piece of your chosen color into a ball the size of a cherry. For the nose, use another small piece of clay the same color. Roll it into a short sausage shape and place it on the head.

3 Press the eyes gently into the face. Push them in carefully with a toothpick to keep from getting your fingerprints all over the face. Use the toothpick to make small dents at the outside edges of each eye to give this guy some expression (photo 1).

What You Need

- Polymer clay:
  1 ounce of whatever color you want the wizard to be
  ½ ounce of black, white, purple, blue, and green
- Aluminum foil
- Approximately 20 inches of craft wire
- Fat knitting needle
- Glitter (optional)
- Craft knife
- Toothpicks
- Blunt pencil or dowel
- Small star cutter

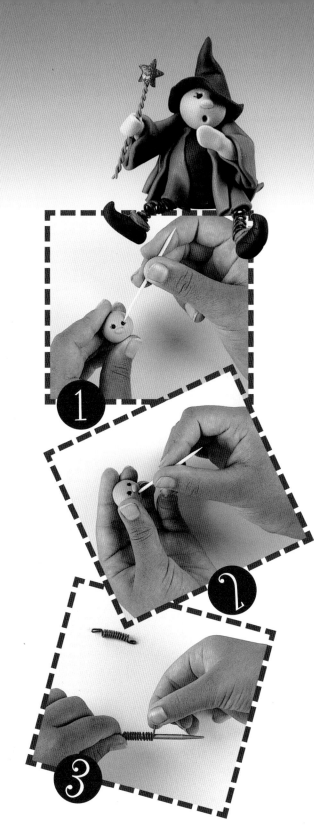

4 Now for a mouth. You can vary the expression a lot by altering the shape and position of the mouth. Poke a hole with the toothpick below the nose, and rotate the toothpick to enlarge the mouth (see photo 2 on page 105). Set the head aside.

5 Now for some springy legs. Cut two pieces of wire, each about 8 inches long. Curl each one around a fat knitting needle, leaving about ½ inch uncurled on each end (see photo 3 on page 105). Fold a little bit over at each end so that the wire will stick better when it's embedded in the clay. Set them aside.

6 Finally it's time to make the wizard's body. Get a piece of aluminum foil about 4 inches wide, and crumple it in your hands. Crush it into a bell shape (wider and flat at the bottom). Flatten a ball of purple clay into a circular sheet. Set the aluminum foil onto the center of the purple clay circle, and smooth the clay upward to cover the bell shape (photo 4). Trim away any excess clay.

7 Use the toothpick to poke two holes in the bottom near the front edge where the wire legs will be inserted. Stick one folded end of each wire leg into a hole, and smooth the clay around the opening.

8 Break a toothpick in half, and poke one of the halves into the top of the body. Leave it sticking out a bit so it can hold the head. Gently push the head down onto the end of the toothpick, and press it firmly to the body (photo 5).

9 Cut a piece of wire about as long as your index finger for the wand. Fold it in half and twist together. Trim the ends. Sandwich one end between two tiny clay stars (photo 6), and dab glitter on the stars with your finger. Set the unclothed wizard and the wand onto some polyester batting on your baking surface, and bake for 20 minutes.

10 For the cape, flatten a ball of green clay into a circle that's about one-and-a-half times as wide as your index finger is long. Cut a triangle out of the circle (like cutting a piece of pie), and drape the rest of the circle around the baked wizard's shoulders, leaving a gap in front to show the purple robe. Pinch folds in the robe, and arrange it around the body (photo 7).

11 For arms, roll two pieces of that skin-colored clay into short logs about as thick as a pencil and half as long as your pinky finger. Flatten one end of each to create sort of a paddle on one end for hands (photo 8). Set these aside for just a moment while you make the sleeves.

12 Roll two pieces of green clay, each a little larger than a marble, into cone shapes. Stick a blunt pencil or dowel into the wide end of each, and roll it gently on the table to open up the sleeves (photo 9).

13 Put an arm into each sleeve, and press them gently onto the body (photo 10). Arrange the hands in a pose you like. Put the wand into one hand, and fold the end of the hand over it.

14 For shoes, roll two small balls of brown clay—each a little smaller than a marble—into cone shapes, and set them aside. Roll two smaller balls of another shade of brown, and push them onto the wide ends of each cone to form socks. Push the socks onto the ends of the wires, and curl up the pointed end of each shoe.

15 The hat is the last part! Roll a ball of blue clay the size of a marble into a cone shape, and open it up with a dowel like you did for the sleeves. Roll a smaller ball of purple into a skinny log, and stick it all around the bottom of the cone to form a brim. Pinch and flatten the brim all around the hat, and put it on the wizard's head (photo 11). It should be big and floppy, and you can tip the point over if you want.

16 Set the dressed wizard onto the batting or rag on your baking sheet and bake for 30 minutes.

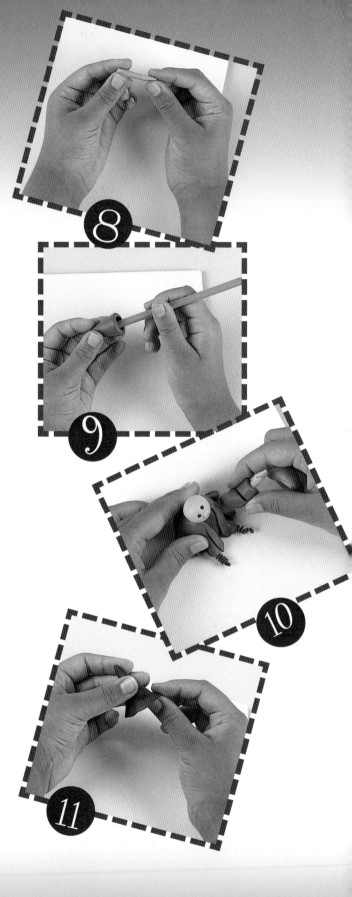

Templates

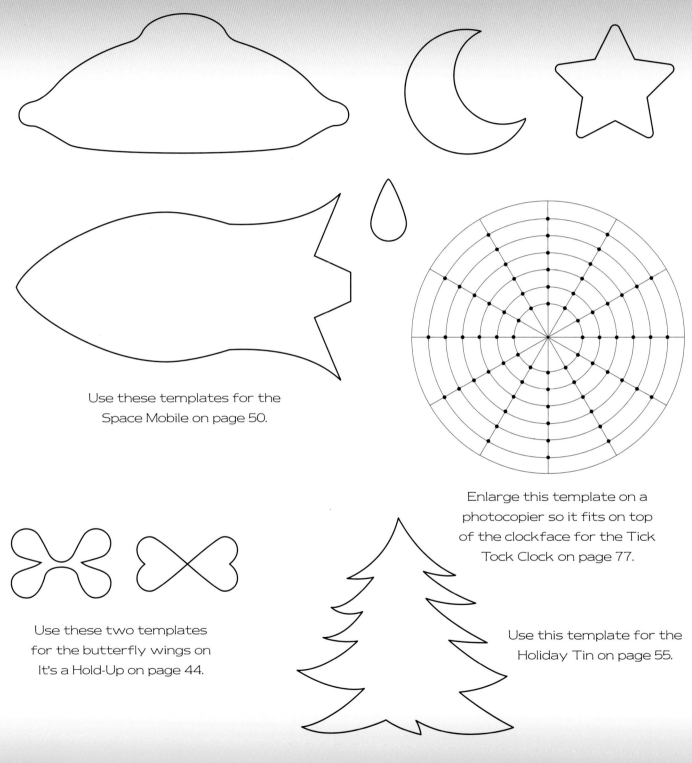

Use these templates for the
Space Mobile on page 50.

Enlarge this template on a
photocopier so it fits on top
of the clockface for the Tick
Tock Clock on page 77.

Use these two templates
for the butterfly wings on
It's a Hold-Up on page 44.

Use this template for the
Holiday Tin on page 55.

Metric Table

Inches	Centimeters	Inches	Centimeters
1/8	3 mm	12	30
1/4	6 mm	13	32.5
3/8	9 mm	14	35
1/2	1.3	15	37.5
5/8	1.6	16	40
3/4	1.9	17	42.5
7/8	2.2	18	45
1	2.5	19	47.5
1 1/4	3.1	20	50
1 1/2	3.8	21	52.5
1 3/4	4.4	22	55
2	5	23	57.5
2 1/2	6.25	24	60
3	7.5	25	62.5
3 1/2	8.8	26	65
4	10	27	67.5
4 1/2	11.3	28	70
5	12.5	29	72.5
5 1/2	13.8	30	75
6	15	31	77.5
7	17.5	32	80
8	20	33	82.5
9	22.5	34	85
10	25	35	87.5
11	27.5	36	90

Multiply ounces by 28 to get grams.
Subtract 32 from Fahrenheit temperature, and then multiply by .56 to get degrees in Celsius.

Designers

Irene Semanchuk Dean

Not only did I write this book, but I also did the following projects: Novel Knobs on page 25, Marbelous Ornaments on page 28, Makin' Faces Switch Plates on page 30, Prehistoric Pencil Cup on page 52, Big Fat Pen on page 69, Tick Tock Clock on page 77, Fine-Feathered Friends on page 80, Bodacious Bauble Bowl on page 84, and Spirit Doll on page 90.
www.good-night-irene.com

Julia Sober

Julia designed the Tic Tac Toe project on page 66.

Julia is a part-time mixed-media artist and teacher living in Rockford, Illinois. She discovered the joys of polymer clay in 1991. She is serving her second term as president of the Chicago Area Polymer Clay Guild, and loves welcoming new people to the fascinating and diverse world of polymer clay.
<jsober@rocketmail.com>

Gerri Newfry

Gerri made the Accordion Book on page 47 and the Locker Mirror on page 94.

Gerri has been working with polymer clay for 11 years. She is a founding member of the Chicago Area Polymer Clay Guild. She especially enjoys integrating polymer clay and book arts, and she currently sells her work on-line at http://www.newfry.com.

Johnny Kuborssy

Johnny made the Plant Critters on page 62.

He's an artist who began working with polymer clay about eight years ago. Johnny is currently the president of the South Bay Polymer Clay Guild in San Jose, California.
<JKuborssy@aol.com>

Debbie Kreuger

Debbie created the Holiday Tin on page 55, as well as Beetlemania on page 58.

Debbie has been working with polymer clay for 13 years. She sells her work in various art and fine craft shows. Teaching others how to play with clay started at home with her two daughters.
<dbriank@aol.com>

Hey look! These project designers were kids once, too!

110

Diane Villano

Diane designed the Space Mobile on page 50.

Diane is the founding president of the Southern Connecticut Polymer Clay Guild and teaches and exhibits her work nationally. Her designs have appeared in periodicals and books, including *The Weekend Crafter: Polymer Clay* by Irene Semanchuk Dean (Lark Books) and *Making Beautiful Beads* (Lark Books). Foxon River Design, 1355 North High Street, East Haven, CT 06512.<dianev_scpcg@yahoo.com>

Elizabeth Campbell

Elizabeth created Hold the Pickles on page 87, Flower Power Vase on page 97, and the Computer Monitor Wizard on page 104.

Elizabeth is the web designer for Polymer Clay Express, and she enjoys designing projects that will help other artists and crafters find their own starting points. <elizabeth@thepolyparrot.com>

Lynn Krucke

Lynn made It's a Hold-Up on page 44, Framed! on page 72, and the Forget-You-Not Bracelet on page 100.

Lynn works with rubber stamps, paper, beads and wire, fabric, fiber, and (of course) polymer clay. Her favorite projects incorporate techniques from more than one medium. Lynn's designs have been featured in books on card making, beading, clocks, glass painting, candles, polymer clay, and wearable art. She lives in Summerville, South Carolina. <lkrucke@bellsouth.net>

Jenny Bezingue

Jenny designed the Witch's Cauldron on page 33, the Marbled Pendant on page 74, and Doughnut Designs on page 36.

Jenny first touched polymer clay more than 10 years ago. She has helped many friends and relatives begin to play with clay, including her 10-year-old nephew, John, and seven-year-old niece, Cathy. Jenny is a founding member of the Chicago Area Polymer Clay Guild, and has won both local and national awards for her polymer clay art and beadwork. <jennybez@earthlink.net>

Georgana Gersabeck

Georgana made the Pushpinzzzzzzzz on page 38, as well as the Window Clings on page 41.

Georgana began creating with polymer clay in 1993. She's participated in arts and crafts shows and is Vice President of the Metropolitan Detroit Polymer Art Guild. She enjoys combining polymer clay with found objects in her artwork. <geogersabeck@home.com>

Index

A Note About Suppliers

Usually, the supplies you need for making the projects in Lark Books can be found at your local craft supply store, discount mart, home improvement center, or retail shop relevant to the topic of the book. Occasionally, however, you may need to buy materials or tools from specialty suppliers. In order to provide you with the most up-to-date information, we have created suppliers listings on our Web site, which we update on a regular basis. Visit us at www.larkbooks.com, click on "Craft Supply Sources," and then click on the relevant topic. You will find numerous companies listed with their web address and/or mailing address and phone number.